W9-BYF-686

Life Signs

*find the opening
to the Grand Canyon of God*

A Retreat with Henri Nouwen

Other titles in the A Retreat With... *Series:*

Mary of Magdala and Augustine: Rejoicing in Human Sexuality,
by Sidney Callahan

Matthew: Going Beyond the Law, by Leslie J. Hoppe, O.F.M.

Mother Teresa and Damien of Molokai: Caring for Those Who Suffer,
by Joan Guntzelman

Oscar Romero and Dorothy Day: Walking With the Poor,
by Marie Dennis

Our Lady of Guadalupe and Juan Diego: Heeding the Call,
by Virgilio Elizondo and Friends

Our Lady, Dominic and Ignatius: Praying With Our Bodies, by
Betsey Beckman, Nina O'Connor and J. Michael Sparough, S.J.

Patrick: Discovering God in All, by Timothy Joyce, O.S.B.

Pope John Paul II: Be Not Afraid, by Jack Wintz, O.F.M.

Pope John XXIII: Opening the Windows to Wisdom, by Alfred
McBride, O. Praem.

Teresa of Avila: Living by Holy Wit, by Gloria Hutchinson

Thea Bowman and Bede Abram: Leaning On the Lord,
by Joseph A. Brown, S.J.

Therese of Lisieux: Loving Our Way Into Holiness,
by Elizabeth Ruth Obbard, O.D.C.

Thomas Merton: Becoming Who We Are, by Dr. Anthony T.
Padovano

A Retreat With Henri Nouwen

Reclaiming Our Humanity

Robert Durback

ST. ANTHONY MESSENGER PRESS

Cincinnati, Ohio

Excerpts from *Man's Search for Meaning* by Victor E. Frankl, copyright ©1959, 1962, 1984, 1992 by Viktor E. Frankl reprinted by permission of Beacon Press, Boston. Excerpts from *Befriending Life: Encounters with Henri Nouwen*, edited by Beth Porter with Susan M.S. Brown and Philip Coulter, copyright ©2001 by The Estate of Henri Nouwen; *Wounded Prophet: A Portrait of Henri J.M. Nouwen*, by Michael Ford, copyright ©1999 by Michael Ford; *The Wounded Healer*, by Henri J.M. Nouwen, copyright ©1972 by Henri J.M. Nouwen; *A Cry for Mercy* by Henri J.M. Nouwen, copyright ©1981 by Henri J.M. Nouwen; *The Road to Daybreak* by Henri Nouwen, copyright ©1988 by Henri J.M. Nouwen; *Conjectures of a Guilty Bystander* by Thomas Merton, copyright ©1966 by The Abbey of Gethsemani; *Lifesigns* by Henri J.M. Nouwen, copyright ©1986 by Henri J.M. Nouwen; *The Return of the Prodigal Son* by Henri Nouwen, copyright ©1992 by Henri J.M. Nouwen; and *The Inner Voice of Love* by Henri Nouwen, copyright ©1996 by Henri Nouwen used by permission of Doubleday, a division of Random House, Inc. Excerpts from *Talmud and the Internet* by Jonathan Rosen, copyright ©2000 by Jonathan Rosen, reprinted by permission of Farrar, Straus and Giroux, LLC. Excerpt from *On Becoming a Person* by Carl R. Rogers, copyright ©1961 and renewed 1989 by Carl R. Rogers, reprinted by permission of Houghton Mifflin Company. Excerpts from *A Dictionary of Quotes from the Saints* by Paul Thigpen copyright ©2000 by Paul Thigpen used with permission of Servant Publications, P.O. Box 8617, Ann Arbor, Michigan 48107. www.servantpub.com. Excerpts from *The Solace of Fierce Landscapes* by Belden C. Lane, copyright ©1988 by Belden C. Lane used by permission of Oxford University Press. Excerpts from *St. Maximilian Kolbe, Apostle of Our Difficult Age* by Antonio Ricciardi reprinted by permission of Pauline Books & Media. Excerpts from *The Psalms*, Grail translation, 1993 revision, copyright ©1993 by Ladies of the Grail (England) are used by permission of GIA Publications, Inc., exclusive agent. All rights reserved.

Scripture citations, unless otherwise indicated, are taken from *New Revised Standard Version Bible,* copyright ©1989 by the Division of Christian Education of the National Council of the Churches of Christ in the U.S.A., and used by permission. All rights reserved.

Cover illustration by Steve Erspamer, S.M.
Cover and book design by Mark Sullivan

ISBN 0-86716-549-9
Copyright © 2003, Robert Durback
All rights reserved.

Library of Congress Cataloging-in-Publication Data

Durback, Robert.
 A retreat with Henri Nouwen : reclaiming our humanity / Robert Durback.
      p. cm. – (Retreat with—series)
Includes bibliographical references.
 ISBN 0-86716-549-9 (alk. paper)
 1. Spiritual retreat—Catholic Church. 2. Nouwen, Henri J. M. I. Title. II. Series.
 BX2375.D87 2003
 269'.6—dc22
                                        2003017631

Published by St. Anthony Messenger Press
www.AmericanCatholic.org
Printed in the U.S.A.

To Francis Kline and the monks of Mepkin Abbey whose warm and nurturing hospitality provided the sacred space and fertile ground from which the insights born in this retreat could come to full flower.

Contents

Acknowledgments

When I received a call from Kathleen Carroll at St. Anthony Messenger Press, asking if I would contribute to the *A Retreat With...* series by preparing *A Retreat With Henri Nouwen*, I was not only surprised, but felt very honored. My first word of thanks must go to Kathleen and also to Lisa Biedenbach, Editorial Director of Books at St. Anthony Messenger Press, not only for their kind invitation, but for their enthusiastic support and encouragement throughout the months of waiting and working on the book.

I realized from the start that to write a book of this nature, the first thing I would have to do would be to go into retreat! My mind traveled quickly to Mepkin Abbey in South Carolina, where I had lived as a monk for over nine years, from 1954 to 1964. So I sat down and wrote a letter to Abbot Francis Kline, explaining my situation and asking if I could make Mepkin Abbey my home for the duration of my "book retreat." His response was quick and most supportive, which filled me with joy and gratitude. Weeks later I moved myself and my Nouwen library to Mepkin Abbey, and from late March through December, 2002, plunged headlong into pursuing the theme I had chosen—of reclaiming our humanity in a technological age—with Henri Nouwen as my guide.

With my task completed, I am happy to dedicate this book to Francis Kline and the Mepkin community, whose generosity provided every convenience and tool friendly to my task of compiling the book, including access to the monastery's newly completed library and the graced companionship of Brother Callistus Crichlow, who not only gave freely of his technical expertise when needed, but warmed my heart with his Christed presence. For help in the editing process I turned to Jeanne Koma, my mainstay for years, who devoted hours to combing the text carefully and offering suggestions which greatly improved the text. Michael O'Laughlin, who was Nouwen's teaching assistant at Harvard, not only devoted hours to critiquing my text and offering valuable suggestions, but also gave permission to incorporate some of his own unique perspectives on Nouwen's thinking into the text of this retreat. Christian Carr of Mepkin, also my mentor over many years, rendered the indispensable service of seeing to it that not only my thought, but also my punctuation was impeccable throughout.

I would never submit commentary on Nouwen's writings for publication without clearing it first with Sue Mosteller, who was, perhaps, the person closest to Henri in the last ten years of his life. I am so grateful for the love and encouragement with which she has blessed me every step of the way in my work on this retreat. Maureen Wright and Mary Lou Daquano at the Henri Nouwen Literary Center and Gabrielle Earnshaw at the Nouwen Archives in Toronto keep me well informed on all matters Nouwenesque. I welcome the opportunity to tell them how much I appreciate their friendship and support.

I reserve my final words of gratitude for Brothers Stan Gumula and John Corrigan, who stretched their administration resources to provide the space for me to meet my deadlines. For your many years of friendship and the warm hospitality of the Mepkin community at large I can only express my deepest gratitude for the privilege of spending these precious months in your midst.

Robert Durback
Christmas Eve, 2002
Mepkin Abbey, Moncks Corner, S.C.

Introducing A Retreat With...

Several years ago, Gloria Hutchinson took up the exhortation once given to Thomas Merton: "Keep on writing books that make people love the spiritual life." Through her own writing and that of many gifted others, Gloria brought flesh and format to this retreat series.

It is with a deep appreciation for her foresight in laying the groundwork that I have assumed the role of series editor. Those of you who have returned to this series again and again will not be jarred by the changes; they are few and subtle. Those of you who are new will find, I hope, that God works to reach us in any manner we will permit, if we but take the time to come aside for a while and wait for the spirit.

The many mentors who have come to life in the pages of this series are not meant to be a conglomeration of quotes by and about them. They are intimate portraits, drawn by authors who know their subject well. But just as our viewing of the Mona Lisa tells us more about ourselves than about Leonardo's relationship with his mysterious subject, so the real value in these retreats comes from the minds and the hearts of their readers. You are invited to dream and doubt, muse and murmur. If you find a mentor's words compelling, the end of each book has a list of resources to deepen your acquaintance. If you find some of your mentor's ideas challenging, or even disturbing, you can be sure the spirit is at work.

Come aside for a while...

Kathleen Carroll
Series Editor

Getting to Know Our Director

Jonathan Rosen, in his engaging memoir, *The Talmud and the Internet*, sums up the state of the world in which we live today:

> I understand better now than I ever did that I live in a society which, for all its outward comforts, is in a constant state of recovery from the shattering upheavals of the century just past. My father's father fought in—and survived—the First World War, a conflict that killed nine million soldiers. In the Second World War he was taken from his home and murdered, one of the six million Jews and fifty million human beings destroyed by a war that did not distinguish between soldiers and civilians. I cannot say I know how to fit my own private ghosts into the terrible tally of the twentieth century, when whole populations and whole belief systems perished. But I do understand now that my own life is part of that aftermath. I do not need to conjure an artificial crisis. It's the *response* I need to figure out.[1]

It was into this world that Henri Jozef Machiel Nouwen was born on January 24, 1932, in the small village of Nijkerk, some twenty-eight miles southeast of Amsterdam in Holland. By the time he was of school age, one of his first lessons would be found in observing the skill of his father in hiding from the occupying forces of Germany. Because of the war his grandparents had moved in with the family.

He vividly recalls the harrowing incident after D-Day when German soldiers forced their way into his parents' home, seeking to take his father into forced labor. His father, Laurent, knowing the danger that surrounded his family daily, had carved out a hiding place for himself beneath a windowsill in the attic. He remained there in hiding for entire days, reading by candlelight, always in suspense over a possible sudden incursion by Nazi soldiers, never certain whose footsteps he heard outside his hiding place. When soldiers finally did make their way into the home, there was no way for his family to signal to him to stay concealed. When he heard the accustomed footsteps outside his hiding place under the windowsill, he was about to emerge to take the food he thought his father was bringing him but wisely followed his instinct that told him to remain silent until spoken to. The soldiers looked carefully around the room, found no one, and left the house. His obedience to his instinct saved him from captivity.[2]

Though the war was disruptive in many ways, Maria Nouwen was determined that her son's schooling would not be interrupted. She recruited a group of young priests and convinced them to create their own school in the neighboring village. In this way Henri and six other classmates were able to continue their elementary education without interruption.

From his earliest years Nouwen admired his uncle who was a priest and decided early on that he too would someday become a priest. So taken was he with the idea that he played "priest" in his home, wearing vestments his grandmother had made for him and "celebrating Mass," ordering his younger brothers to serve at his Mass, and distributing wafer communions to his young friends and family members during his solemn high pontifications. The family photo album is well stocked with photos of the child Henri garbed in his priestly vestments and devoutly ministering to a captive audience of family communicants.

At eighteen he was ready to enter the seminary. After one year in the minor seminary where his uncle was rector, he went on to the major seminary in Utrecht, where he remained from 1951 until ordination in 1957. His leadership skills, already well honed, were reflected in his popularity with his fellow students and his eventual election as president of the entire student body. He was popular, but scholarship as such held little appeal for him. His interest throughout his years of study was focused on practical aspects of pastoral ministry. Henri Nouwen was always people oriented.

A biographer, Jurjen Beumer, noting Nouwen's penchant to explore new and unusual options, relates how he joined a work placement program in the mines of South Limburg and another in Rotterdam, adding: "He wanted to know and experience what faith meant in the harsh reality of everyday life."[3] In this move Nouwen was following in the footsteps of Vincent Van Gogh, who would become one of the major spiritual influences in his life.

A turning point came when, upon completion of his seminary studies, Nouwen was asked by his bishop, later to become Cardinal Bernard Alfrink, to study theology. He asked the bishop if he would reconsider and allow him instead to pursue psychology. It would be difficult to overstate the significance of this desire to specialize in psychology rather than theology. Far from being indicative of a disregard for theology, it points rather to a passion for which he would later be so well known: his ability and desire to meet people at their own level, to communicate theological truths in terms ordinary people could understand.

The request was granted. Nouwen was permitted to begin psychological studies at the University of Nijmegen, where he remained from 1957 to 1964. During this period he made the first of many trips to the United States as chaplain on the Holland-American line and eventually began to explore the possibility of pursuing studies in psychology at Harvard under Gordon Allport. Allport convinced him that given his interest in pastoral counseling, he would do better to complete his studies at Nijmegen and then take advantage of an excellent program in psychiatry and religion offered at the Menninger Clinic in Topeka, Kansas.

Nouwen followed Allport's advice and went on to Menninger, where he remained from 1964 to 1966, involving himself in clinical-pastoral education, research and writing. There he made friends with Dr. John Dos Santos, who opened yet another door. Dos Santos was invited to begin a psychology department at the University of Notre Dame. Dos Santos invited Nouwen to join him for a one-year teaching appointment. Later, upon the insistence of Father Theodore Hesburgh, Notre Dame's president, he agreed to remain longer, extending his stay another year, to 1968.

Nouwen liked Notre Dame. He quickly made friends and forged relationships that would be long-lasting. But he also began to realize that he would not be happy simply as a psychologist. He was more interested in priestly formation and ministry. In 1968 he returned to Holland for a three-year stay. During the first two years he taught pastoral psychology and spirituality to students preparing for the ordained ministry. The third year he spent working for a degree in theology at the University of Nijmegen.

In 1970 he received a letter that was to move him in yet another direction. Yale University was inviting him to come for a visit. He accepted the invitation, unaware that upon arrival he would be interviewed and pressed to join the faculty. Attractive though the offer was, Nouwen politely turned it down, affirming his commitment to the church in Holland. The issue was settled once and for all, so it seemed.

Six months later there was another letter asking him to reconsider and to accept a position on the faculty at Yale. He returned to Yale for a second visit and was impressed by the caliber and healthy mix of students from many different denominations. This time he accepted the teaching position with the approval of his bishop in Holland. Remaining at Yale from 1971 to 1981, he was eventually made full professor of pastoral theology.

Of particular significance during the Yale years were two sabbaticals spent by special arrangement in a Trappist monastery in upstate New York. As a result of his close friendship with the abbot, Dom John Eudes Bamberger, Nouwen was given the unusual opportunity to live for seven months as an integrated member of the monastic community of the Abbey of the Genesee. From this period came two important works, *Genesee Diary* and *A Cry for Mercy,* of which more will be said later.

Nouwen was happy at Yale. His lectures were well-attended. He was popular with his students and sought out as a counselor. But he was never one to settle with complacency into a comfortable position. A long-standing interest in the affairs of Latin America kept him on the road, commuting between two continents. This concern reached a climax when, feeling compelled by an inner voice, he gave up his prestigious position at Yale to live among the poor in the barrios of Lima, Peru.

In July of 1981 he submitted his resignation from his tenured position at Yale and began preparations to spend six months in Bolivia and Peru. Through the Maryknoll missionary community he arranged to spend three months devoted to improving his Spanish by study in Bolivia, and the remaining three months as a missionary "in the field" among the poor of Peru. His underlying intent was to discern his vocation. He sought an answer to the question: "Does God call me to live and work in Latin America in the years to come?" Out of this experience emerged *Gracias! A Latin American Journal.*

In the end, Nouwen did not opt to become a missionary to Latin America, but the picture he paints and the questions he raises in the journal recording his impressions during his six-month stay make informative, challenging reading, especially for readers accustomed to First World amenities.

In March 1982 he returned to the United States and took up residency in private living quarters made available to him on the grounds of Genesee Abbey. Shortly thereafter, letters began arriving from Harvard asking him to consider taking a position on the faculty there. Nouwen responded that he no longer wished to teach full time at the university level. A compromise was reached in an agreement that he would teach only one semester a year at Harvard and be free for the second half of the year to pursue other interests, particularly in Latin America.

Nouwen moved to Cambridge in the late fall to prepare for his first teaching semester at Harvard in January 1983. When that semester of teaching ended he embarked on another tour of Latin America, traveling first to Mexico, where he stayed for a month. While in Mexico he received an invitation from a Maryknoll missioner to visit Nicaragua. He accepted and soon found himself in the dangerous militarized zone on the border between Nicaragua and Honduras, meeting with peasants, listening to their stories, praying with them, and promising them he would return to the United States to tell his fellow North Americans what he had heard and seen of the hardships and agony of his brothers and sisters in troubled Central America.

Returning to the United States, he promptly launched a far-flung, six-week lecture tour, during which he delivered impassioned accounts of the plight of war-torn, persecuted Nicaraguans and Hondurans, who often were wounded and put to death by weapons provided by the U.S. government.

Following his tour, Nouwen received an invitation to visit Jean Vanier, founder of the L'Arche community for the mentally handicapped in France. Nouwen welcomed the invitation and stayed six weeks. He returned in the fall of the following year to make a thirty-day retreat under the direction of Jesuit Pére André de Jaer. The two visits marked another turning point in his spiritual journey.

Jean Vanier had been a professor of philosophy at St. Michael's College in Toronto when, in 1964, with the encouragement of his spiritual director, Pére Thomas Philippe, o.p., he made the decision to leave the academic world and invited two mentally handicapped men to move into his home and form a household with him. Hearing of his move, it was not long before others asked to join him. Soon more households were formed. Eventually, volunteers began arriving from other countries, offering to live as assistants to the handicapped and to share their knowledge of various handcrafts. A new movement was born.

Today L'Arche has become an international federation numbering over one hundred communities. They are spread throughout France, Britain, Ireland, Italy, Spain, Belgium, Switzerland, Denmark, India, Australia, the Ivory Coast, Burkina Fasso, the West Bank, Haiti, Honduras, Mexico, the Dominican Republic, Brazil, Canada and the United States.

After his time in France, Nouwen returned to his post at Harvard for his third semester, but found it increasingly difficult to work and minister in a purely academic environment. Harvard was not much to his liking. He sensed that his own spiritual life was in danger there, and within weeks of semester's end he submitted his resignation.

Soon after Nouwen had left Harvard he was invited by Jean Vanier to return to L'Arche in France for a longer stay. This time it was suggested that he stay for a year. Nouwen received the invitation as a call from God. He was ready to respond. By late August he was aboard a jet, headed once again for France.

From August 1985 to August 1986 Nouwen familiarized himself with the world of the handicapped, eating with them, playing with them, working with them, and above all, learning from them. He committed his experiences to writing in a new journal which was published as *The Road to Daybreak*.

Daybreak is the name of the Toronto branch of L'Arche, founded in 1969. It is a large community. Inevitably his involvement with L'Arche led Nouwen to make a brief visit to the Daybreak community. It was not long after his visit that he received a letter inviting him to join the community at Daybreak as pastor. Nouwen discerned this a further call from God. With the approval of the cardinal archbishop in Holland he accepted the invitation and pledged himself to a three-year commitment to the Daybreak community. As it turned out, he would remain for ten years, until the day of his death.

The Writer

Henri Nouwen does not write as a philosopher king. He is better understood if compared with a war reporter writing from the trenches next to the infantrymen, with mortars lighting up the crowded space in which he hurriedly takes notes. Nouwen writes from life lived in the raw. I believe it is safe to say that it is this quality of intensity and authenticity that explains the exceptional appeal his books have had with readers for more than thirty years since the publication of his first book in the United States in 1969.

One may wonder how the busy and well-traveled Nouwen found time to do any writing! Since he published over forty books, there is ample evidence that he did indeed find time to write. It is important, nevertheless, to note that before he was a writer he was a speaker. Bob Massie, a close friend of Nouwen's, describes Nouwen's lively gestures as a speaker:

> His fingers were as much an instrument of
> communication as his voice; they were a
> ten-member liturgical dance corps that
> performed in front of him whenever he
> opened his mouth. He spoke, and they
> swirled through the air, coming together
> in reverence, flinging apart in exuberance....
> When I saw Henri in his coffin, I felt the
> physical reality of his death not just
> because his face was quiet and his eyes
> closed but because his hands were still.[4]

Nouwen's writing career began almost by accident, indeed an embarrassing one: In the late sixties he was invited to give a summer course at the University of Notre Dame. But after his arrival he found that the program had been canceled for lack of response. Nouwen found himself a lecturer without an audience. The administration had to find something for him to do. They asked him to give a lecture to a conference of priests at Notre Dame.

Nouwen was in his element. An evening lecture was scheduled. The response was overwhelming. After the lecture Nouwen was approached by a stringer from *National Catholic Reporter.* The reporter asked Nouwen for a copy of the lecture. Nouwen complied, and it was rushed into print. The article unleashed a landslide of reader response. More articles were solicited and began to appear in series in *National Catholic Reporter* as they came fresh off of Nouwen's desk. Nouwen's literary career was launched. By 1969 his lectures and writings, focusing on various aspects of psychology and spirituality, were ready to be compiled in book form under the title *Intimacy: Pastoral Psychological Essays.* The book caught the attention of Colin Williams, Dean of Yale University, and Nouwen was targeted for recruitment to the faculty of the Yale Divinity School.

For a summary review of the complete collection of Nouwen's books I refer readers to my book, *Seeds of Hope: A Henri Nouwen Reader* with its complete annotated bibliography[5] and by all means, the Henri Nouwen Website: www.nouwen.net. For our retreat we will focus attention on selected works of particular interest. One of Nouwen's earliest works, *With Open Hands,* first published in Dutch and translated into English for Ave Maria Press in 1972, continues to draw readers with short, probing reflections on prayer in the context of daily living. Enhanced with photographs, it invites readers to pause and reflect, to mine the hidden substratum of possibilities for prayer waiting to be discovered in the context of the most ordinary situations in life.

Reaching Out: The Three Movements of the Spiritual Life, written during Nouwen's earlier years at Yale, is one of his most carefully crafted works, foundational to much of his thought in the years to follow. Nouwen gives his own evaluation in the introduction: "...closer to me than anything I have written and tries to articulate my most personal thoughts and feelings about being a Christian."

The three movements are: from loneliness to solitude, from hostility to hospitality, from illusion to prayer. They are neatly summed up by Deirdre LaNoue as three basic relationships in the life of every Christian: relationship to God: "To Whom Do I Belong?," relationship to self: "Who Am I?" and relationship to others: "What Is My Purpose?"[6]

Given its attention to the theme that is to guide us in this retreat, *Wounded Healer* deserves special mention. It offers Nouwen's vision of the role and self-understanding required of the Christian leader in a nuclear age. Written during the same period, *Creative Ministry* serves well as a companion volume, charting the course for new and innovative approaches to pastoral leadership that are called for in a rapidly changing world.

Four journals stand in a category of their own: *Genesee Diary, Gracias! A Latin American Journal, Road to Daybreak* and *Sabbatical Journey.* Each records Nouwen's continual search to find where God might be calling him to make radical changes in his life: The first, *Genesee Diary,* chronicles his seven-month sabbatical in a Trappist monastery at a time when he was questioning his position as tenured professor in the competitive environment he found at Yale; *Gracias! A Latin American Journal,* is the record of his six-month experience of training for missionary work in Bolivia and living among the poor in Peru after resigning his position at Yale.

The Road to Daybreak marks yet another turning point. Making a definitive break with the academic world, and having found he could not live as a missionary in Latin America, Nouwen documents the events that lead him finally to embrace a call to work among the mentally and physically handicapped as pastor of the community of

L'Arche Daybreak in Toronto. In his own words: "It is a screaming and kicking 'yes' that fills these pages."

Nouwen joined the community at Daybreak in August of 1986. On September 1, 1995, the community granted him a sabbatical, hoping it would free him to do what he did best: write. And write he did. *Sabbatical Journey* is the journal he kept while he was working on four other books. He completed three of them. On September 21, 1996, three weeks after returning from his sabbatical, Nouwen died of a heart attack in Hilversum, Holland, while en route to Russia to do a telecast for Dutch TV. Being the fourth and last of his journals, *Sabbatical Journey* claims a special place among Nouwen's writings, an unwittingly final *adieu* to his readers.

The Henri Nouwen Effect

Reading Henri Nouwen is not only informative, it is transformative. By telling us his story he invites us to revisit our own stories—especially those areas we may have avoided for fear of the painful memories we may find stored up in our inner attics and closets. Nouwen, by his honesty and directness, reveals to us the healing that can be found by letting in the light of God's presence, which exposes not only our vulnerabilities, but also the warmth of God's love, God's sustaining compassion and desire to clothe us anew as the Father in the Gospel story so extravagantly outfitted the returning prodigal.

If I were to recommend a single book out of the entire Nouwen collection as a "must" to be read as a companion or follow up to this seven-day retreat, it would be *The Inner Voice of Love: A Journey Through Anguish to Freedom.*[7] Many, including this reader, would rate *The Return of the Prodigal Son* as Nouwen's crowning achievement. But for starters, *Inner Voice of Love* is doable—a slim volume with pithy reflections in short segments. Both books emerge from a period of deep struggle in Nouwen's life and complement one another.

The Inner Voice of Love is a collection of "spiritual imperatives," as Nouwen calls them, sixty-two in all, a rich resource of wisdom. The imperatives are short, incisive, finely honed statements, averaging one to two pages in length. "Silver bullets," one might call them, aimed to pierce to the core of the human heart. In his introduction Nouwen wisely cautions the reader: "Do not read too many of these imperatives at once! They were written over a long period of time and need to be read that way too.... These spiritual imperatives are meant to be like salt for the meal of your life. Too much salt might spoil it, but a little at a time can make it tasty!"

Good advice. This book is best read one segment at a time, offering the reader a theme for reflection for the day. The sixty-two imperatives might well be called: "Sixty-Two Ways of Reclaiming Your Humanity."

If there is one word that sums up a distinctive strain running throughout all Nouwen's writings, it is *enabler*. Nouwen is the enabler *par excellence*. In claiming his self-understanding as God's Beloved, he enables the reader to claim his or her own self-understanding as God's Beloved. In seeing the poor, the persecuted, the disabled and the outcasts of society as the Beloved of God, he teaches us to be alert to see in the poor, the persecuted, the disabled and the outcasts of society the Beloved of God. In crying out to God in the midst of fierce inner struggles, he inspires his readers to do the same: not to surrender to defeat or self-loathing, but to cry out to God, who stands ready to lift us up out of our dilemmas, our failures and dead ends. In persistently claiming his humanity, Nouwen shows us the way to reclaim our humanity.

Perhaps few have summed up the "Henri Nouwen Effect" as well as Michael O'Laughlin, who served as

Nouwen's teaching assistant during his years at Harvard. Writing in the *Christian Spirituality Bulletin*, O'Laughlin penetrates to the heart of the quintessential Nouwen, to what really made him tick:

> There is…a type in Jungian psychology known as the *Puer Eternus,* the boy who never grows up, and I think that besides being a celebrity, Henri was a *puer*. It was no accident that he went off and joined the circus, which is every child's fantasy. Henri's ability to step free of the careful but monotonous life of mature scholarship and priesthood to live in a world of his own making was very *puer*-like. I am not saying that Henri did not grow or change. He was always reaching towards new and higher levels of authenticity and expression. I am also in awe of his 18-hour work days. But, deep down, Henri remained a boy, particularly in close friendships. In fact, for me he was a lot like Peter Pan, a figure who appears at your bedside to tell you that you can fly away with him, if only you submit to his enchantment and his charm. Henri left the details and the follow-up to others, to the grown-ups; what he offered us was a unique opportunity to really live the spirit of the gospel, to reach out, to really let go. This *puer* or "pan" quality Henri had was at the heart of his ability to enchant his friends and readers.[8]

In these few words O'Laughlin offers a beautiful insight into the rapport Nouwen enjoyed with his readers. As we read his books, we can almost hear Nouwen whispering into our ears: "Do not be content with being grounded all your life! Let me show you how to spread your wings!"

In October, 1980, an honorary doctorate was conferred on Henri Nouwen by Virginia Theological Seminary. Though it expresses in sincere and formal terms the full sweep of the impact of Nouwen's writings, there is an element of playfulness in the clever references to the titles of his books not entirely foreign to the "Peter Pan" image painted in the paragraph above. The citation reads in part:

> For a generation of Christians in search of their lost humanity and a forgotten spirituality, you have found a way out of solitude into creative discipleship and ministry. Few of your contemporaries have managed with such grace and clarity to combine the insights of modern psychology with the ancient truths of biblical religion. As a pastoral theologian your own vital priesthood serves as a living reminder to your colleagues in ministry of the need to help each new generation hear and understand the loving compassion of the Word of God.
>
> Through your books and essays, your published meditations and reflections, you have become one of the most widely read interpreters of the Christian way for seekers and followers in our time. And when you preach and teach the Gospel of God's renewing love in Christ, your hearers know the power of prophecy, evangelism, and the priestly cure of souls.
>
> Born and bred in the old world, you are now at home in the new. Baptized and

ordained by the Catholic Church, you are
now at home in many traditions and
communities of the Christian family.
Though a university scholar and
professor, you have discovered the secret
of teaching all sorts and conditions of
searching souls. [9]

We are ready now to explore selected segments of
Nouwen's teachings, in the hope that they will indeed
speak to "all sorts and conditions of searching souls."

Notes

1. Jonathan Rosen, *The Talmud and the Internet, A Journey Between Worlds* (New York: Farrar, Straus and Giroux, 2000), p. 110.

2. I have included a greater amount of biographical material in *Seeds of Hope: A Henri Nouwen Reader, Robert Durback,* ed., 2nd ed. (New York: Doubleday, 1997). Introduction, pp. 21–47.

3. Jurjen Beumer, *Henri Nouwen: A Restless Seeking For God* (New York: Crossroad, 1997), p. 24.

4. *Befriending Life: Encounters With Henri Nouwen,* Beth Porter, Susan M.S. Brown and Philip Coulter, eds. (New York: Doubleday, 2001), p. 10.

5. *Seeds of Hope (Memorial Edition),* Robert Durback, ed. (New York: Doubleday, 1997), bibliography.

6. Deirdre LaNoue, *The Spiritual Legacy of Henri Nouwen* (New York: Continuum, 2000), pp. 59–60.

7. Henri Nouwen, *The Inner Voice of Love: A Journey Through Anguish to Freedom* (New York: Doubleday, 1996).

8. "Flying with the Dutchman: A Review of Two Recent Books About Henri Nouwen", by Michael O'Laughlin, *Christian Spirituality Bulletin,* Fall/Winter, 1999, pp. 24–25.

9. Also quoted in my first edition of *Seeds of Hope: A Henri Nouwen Reader* (New York: Bantam Books, 1989), Introduction, pp. xxxv, xxxvi.

Day One

Reclaiming Our Humanity in a Technological Age

Technology is so far ahead of human relations! There is such a need for new ways for people to be together, to solve conflicts, to work for peace. On the level of human relations, we are still in the Stone Age, thinking that power games and fear tactics will settle our problems. Suicide attacks and military reprisals are such primitive ways to respond to threatening situations. With the technology now at hand, these primitive responses may cause the end of all human life.

More than ever it is necessary for people, who can fly to each other from faraway distances within a few hours, to speak to each other about living together in peace. Now it seems that the smaller the physical distance, the larger the moral and spiritual distance. Why do we human beings learn so much, so soon, about technology, and so little, so late, about loving one another?

—Henri Nouwen[1]

Introducing Our Retreat Theme

In January of 1983, something happened that hadn't happened in fifty-five years of publishing. As the world was waiting for *Time* magazine to name its Man of the Year, *Time* unleashed a surprise: the Man of the Year turned out to be the Machine of the Year. There, on the cover, was not a statesman, pope or president, but the faceless, uncommunicating communicator we call the computer. Human was out. Hardware was in.

The significance of this event reached far beyond the breaking of a fifty-five-year precedent. The preponderance of machine over person marked a rupture between a past generation guided by its respect for personhood and a new generation fascinated by the wonders of technology.

While philosophers and social scientists will be probing the implications of this turnabout for years to come, it is not too soon to make an assessment of the direction the computer revolution has taken to date: The benefits to education, to the economy, to medicine, to the sciences and to society in general are vast indeed. But there is a negative side to technology. Without becoming a progress-denying naysayer, Henri Nouwen bids us pause to reevaluate our mixed blessing.[2]

In *Wounded Healer* Henri Nouwen ponders the predicament of the new nuclear generation:

> Nuclear man is a man who has lost naïve faith in the possibilities of technology and is painfully aware that the same powers that enable man to create new life-styles carry the potential for self-destruction. Let me tell you an old tale of ancient India which might help us to capture the situation of nuclear man:
>
> Four royal sons were questioning what specialty they should master. They said to one another, "Let us search the earth and learn a special science." So they decided, and after they had agreed on a

place where they would meet again, the four brothers started off, each in a different direction. Time went by, and the brothers met again at the appointed meeting place, and they asked one another what they had learned. "I have mastered a science," said the first, "which makes it possible for me, if I have nothing but a piece of bone of some creature, to create straightaway the flesh that goes with it."

"I," said the second, "know how to grow that creature's skin and hair if there is flesh on its bones." The third said, "I am able to create its limbs if I have the flesh, the skin, and the hair." "And I," concluded the fourth, "know how to give life to that creature if its form is complete with limbs."

Thereupon the four brothers went into the jungle to find a piece of bone so that they could demonstrate their specialties. As fate would have it, the bone they found was a lion's, but they did not know that and picked up the bone. One added flesh to the bone, the second grew hide and hair, the third completed it with matching limbs, and the fourth gave the lion life. Shaking its heavy mane, the ferocious beast arose with its menacing mouth, sharp teeth, and merciless claws and jumped on his creators. He killed them all and vanished contentedly into the jungle.[3]

Nouwen concludes: "…the problem is not that the future holds a new danger, such as a nuclear war, but that there might be no future at all." [4]

Sixteen years later Nouwen continues to lament the problems that accompany the benefits of technology:

> Traveling from Paris to Boston made me sharply aware of the contrast between the great advancements in technology and the primitive quality of human relationships. While the most sophisticated machinery took me from Paris to London in one hour and from London to Boston is six hours, the entire trip was clouded by security concerns. More than an hour before the departure of the flight I had to say good-bye to Nathan and Brad, who were with me at Charles de Gaulle Airport in Paris. They were not allowed to be with me while I was checking in my luggage. In London I had to go through countless security checks and a body search and had to identify the luggage that I had asked to be sent directly to Boston. The delays were connected not with technical concerns, but with security problems.
>
> It is obviously a good thing that so many precautions are being taken to prevent terrorist attacks, but the fact that every step of the way you are made aware that someone might try to kill you gives you a sense that the world is a precarious place to live in. The more advanced the method of transportation, the less safe it seems to be transported! Quite a few of my friends have canceled their vacation

plans because of fear of being hijacked, bombed, or attacked on airplanes or in airports.

Technology is so far ahead of human relations! There is such a need for new ways for people to be together, to solve conflicts, to work for peace. On the level of human relations, we are still in the Stone Age, thinking that power games and fear tactics will settle our problems. Suicide attacks and military reprisals are such primitive ways to respond to threatening situations. With the technology now at hand, these primitive responses may cause the end of all human life.

More than ever it is necessary for people, who can fly to each other from faraway distances within a few hours, to speak to each other about living together in peace. Now it seems that the smaller the physical distance, the larger the moral and spiritual distance. Why do we human beings learn so much, so soon, about technology, and so little, so late, about loving one another?[5]

Nouwen pursues this last question at many points throughout his writings, implicitly if not explicitly, but he gives it special attention in *Lifesigns: Intimacy, Fecundity, and Ecstasy in Christian Perspective*. Therefore, during this first day of our retreat we shall listen to Henri Nouwen speak to us about the movement from the house of fear to the house of love, drawing on excerpts from *Lifesigns*. Let us take for our opening prayer the prayer of Henri Nouwen from the collection of prayers in his book, *A Cry For Mercy: Prayers From the Genesee*.

Opening Prayer

O Lord Jesus Christ…Let me recognize you
at that virginal point in the depth of my
heart where you dwell and heal me. Let
me experience you in that center of my
being from which you want to teach and
guide me.... Take away the many fears,
suspicions and doubts by which I prevent
you from being my Lord, and give me the
courage and freedom to appear naked and
vulnerable in the light of your presence,
confident in your unfathomable mercy.[6]

RETREAT SESSION ONE

Moving from the House of Fear

We are fearful people. The more people I
come to know and the more I come to know
people, the more I am overwhelmed by the
negative power of fear. It often seems that
fear has invaded every part of our being to
such a degree that we no longer know what
a life without fear would feel like. There
always seems to be something to fear:
something within us or around us,
something close or far away, something
visible or invisible, something in ourselves,
in others, or in God. There never seems to
be a totally fear-free moment. When we
think, talk, act or react, fear always seems to
be there: an omnipresent force that we
cannot shake off. Often fear has penetrated

our inner selves so deeply that it controls,
whether we are aware of it or not, most of
our choices and decisions.In many, often
very subtle ways fear victimizes and
controls us. Fear can make us upset and
angry. It can drive us into depression or
despair. It can surround us with darkness
and make us make us feel close to
destruction and death. Fear can become so
intolerable that we are willing to do
anything to be relieved from it—even kill
ourselves. It not seldom appears as a cruel
tyrant who takes possession of us and forces
us to live in his house. In fact, most of
us…fear most of the time. It has become an
obvious dwelling place, an acceptable basis
on which to make our decisions and plan
our lives.

But why are we so terribly afraid? Why
is it so hard to find fearless people? Would
there be so much fear if it was not useful to
somebody? I have raised these questions
ever since I became conscious of the
gripping fear in myself and others.
Gradually, I began to see the simple fact that
those I feared had a great power over me.
Those who could make me afraid could also
make me do what they wanted me to do.
People are afraid for many reasons, but I am
convinced that the close connection between
power and fear deserves special attention.

So much power is wielded by instilling
fear in people and keeping them afraid.
There are so many fearful children, fearful
students, fearful patients, fearful employees,

fearful parents, fearful ministers, and fearful
believers. Nearly always, a threatening
figure stands behind them and holds them
under control: a father, a teacher, a doctor, a
boss, a bishop, a church or God. Fear is one
of the most effective weapons in the hands
of those who seek to control us. As long as
we are kept in fear we can be made to act,
speak, and even think as slaves.

The agenda of our world—the issues
and items that fill newspapers and
newscasts—is an agenda of fear and power.
It is amazing, yes frightening, to see how
easily that agenda becomes ours. The things
and people we think about, worry about,
reflect upon, prepare ourselves for, and
spend time and energy on are in large part
determined by a world which seduces us
into accepting its fearful questions. Look at
the many "if" questions we raise: "What am
I going to do if I do not find a spouse, a
house, a job, a friend, a benefactor? What
am I going to do if they fire me, if I get sick,
if an accident happens, if I lose my friend, if
my marriage does not work out, if a war
breaks out?"

A huge network of anxious questions
surrounds us and begins to guide many, if
not most of our daily decisions. Clearly,
those who can pose these fearful questions
which bind us within have true power over
us. For hidden under their questions lies the
threat that not following their directions will
make our worst fears come true. Once we
accept these questions as our own, and are

convinced that we must find answers to them, we become more and more settled in the house of fear.

When we consider how much our educational, political, religious, and even social lives are geared to finding answers to questions born of fear, it is not hard to understand why a message of love has little chance of being heard.

Fearful questions never lead to love-filled answers; underneath every fearful question many other fearful questions are hidden.... [F]ear engenders fear. Fear never gives birth to love.

If this is the case, the nature of the questions we raise is as important as the answers to our questions. Which questions guide our lives? Which questions do we make our own? Which questions deserve our undivided attention and full personal commitment? Finding the right questions is as crucial as finding the right answers....

A careful look at the gospels shows that Jesus seldom accepted the questions posed to him. He exposed them as coming from the house of fear.... He gently put them aside as questions emerging from false worries. They were raised out of concern for prestige, influence, power, and control. They did not belong to the house of God. Therefore Jesus always transformed the question by his answer. He made the question new—and only then worthy of his response.

Though we think of ourselves as followers of Jesus, we are often seduced by the fearful questions the world presents to us. Without fully realizing it, we become anxious, nervous, worrying people caught in the questions of survival: our own survival, the survival of our families, friends and colleagues, the survival of our church, our country, and our world. Once these fearful survival questions become the guiding questions of our lives, we tend to dismiss words spoken from the house of love as unrealistic, romantic, sentimental, pious, or just useless.

...[L]ove is stronger than fear, though it may often seem that the opposite is true. "Perfect love casts out all fear" says St. John in his first letter.... I hope to search for signs of this perfect love and look for ways to follow those signs. I hope to show the possibility of a spiritual movement: the movement out of the house of fear into the house of love.

But is it possible in the midst of this fear-provoking world to live in the house of love and listen there to the questions raised by the Lord of love? Or are we so accustomed to living in fear that we have become deaf to the voice that says: "Do not be afraid."[7]

For Reflection

■ *Nouwen invites us to move from the house of fear to the house of love. Which house do you live in? How long have you lived there? Are you comfortable in this "house"? Would you like to rearrange the furniture? Or move out completely?*

- *Open the Book of Psalms and look for one that gives expression to your own deepest feelings. If you live in the house of fear, look for psalms that speak of fear. If you want to give thanks for the blessings in your life, look for a psalm that speaks of love, praise and thanksgiving.*[8]

- *Consider making it your practice to pray the psalms daily. Fix a special time of the day to which you will be faithful. If circumstances allow, pray the psalms out loud—if you simply read the psalms silently, they remain someone else's prayer. Aloud, they more readily become your own, a cry from your own heart.*

- *Do not confine yourself to a single version of the psalms. There are a number in print, and it is most likely that newer versions will be forthcoming. The advantage of having access to a number of versions is that one can often find small differences—often a single word—that will speak more directly to you as you are praying the psalm.*

- *Keep a bound blank notebook on a table within reach of where you pray. When you find a psalm verse that strikes you in a special way, write it down in your notebook. Watch your treasure grow over the years.*

- *Pray at least one of the psalms from today's Closing Prayer in its entirety. Choose a phrase that strikes you particularly and use it as a mantra throughout the day.*

Closing Prayer

The Lord is my light and my help;
whom shall I fear?
The Lord is the stronghold of my life;
before whom shall I shrink?
Though an army encamp against me

my heart would not fear.
Though war break out against me
even then would I trust.[9]

I sought the Lord and he answered me;
from all my terrors he set me free.[10]

Notes

1. Henri Nouwen. *The Road to Daybreak*, pp. 182–183.

2. Comments on "Machine of the Year" appeared originally in *Praying*, No. 18, 1987, under article entitled: *Henri Nouwen: Spirituality for Our Technological Age*, p. 9.

3. From: *Tales of Ancient India*, translated from the Sanskrit by J.A.B. van Buitenen (New York: Bantam Books, 1961), pp. 50–51.

4. Henri Nouwen, *Wounded Healer*, pp. 5–7.

5. Henri Nouwen, *The Road to Daybreak*, pp. 182–183.

6. Henri Nouwen, *A Cry for Mercy: Prayers from the Genessee* (New York: Doubleday, 2002), p. 24.

7. Henri Nouwen, *Lifesigns* (New York: Doubleday, 1986), pp. 15–21.

8. Of the many versions available, we list here the following: *The Psalms: ICEL Version*, (Chicago: Liturgy Training Publications) and the two listed below in Notes 9 and 10. You may also wish to consult *Psalms For Praying: An Invitation to Wholeness*, by Nan C. Merrill (New York: Continuum, 2000). This is not a translation of the Hebrew Psalms, but rather a modern day "companion" or "dialogue…of one age speaking with a later age," as the author puts it. An alternative for those seeking aids to prayer.

9. Psalm 27:1,3, *The Psalms: Grail Trans.*, 1993 Revision, (Chicago: G.I.A. Publications, 1993), p. 40.

10. Psalm 34:4, *Abbey Psalter* (Mahwah, N.J.: Paulist Press, 1981).

DAY TWO
Listening to a New Voice

Technology can elevate and improve man's life only on one condition: that it remains subservient to his real interests; that it respects his true being; that it remembers that the origin and goal of all is in God. But when technology merely takes over all being for its own purposes, merely exploits and uses up all things in the pursuit of its own ends, and makes everything, including man himself, subservient to its own processes, then it degrades man, despoils the world, ravages life, and leads to ruin.
—Thomas Merton[1]

Coming Together in the Spirit

In our reading for Day One Nouwen laments: "Why do we human beings learn so much, so soon, about technology, and so little, so late, about loving one another?" Speaking about "loving one another" in the context of a discussion on technology may sound naïve, something one might expect to hear from a preacher in church on Sunday, but still peripheral to dealing with the practical aspects of insuring the safety of airports and other areas when the threat of terrorism is very real.

But Nouwen is correct in locating technology within the realm of human relations. Technology does not exist in a vacuum. It is the creation of human hands and can be used either for our benefit or harm. Speaking of love in this context is not a mere sentimentality. It is necessary for survival.

Writing in 1961, psychologist Carl Rogers, whom Nouwen liked to quote, offers a penetrating insight in the introduction to his book, *On Becoming a Person*:

> Man's awesome scientific advances into the infinitude of space as well as the infinitude of sub-atomic particles seems most likely to lead to the total destruction of our world unless we can make great advances in understanding and dealing with interpersonal and inter-group tensions.... I feel very humble about the modest knowledge which has been gained in this field. I hope for the day when we will invest at least the price of one or two large rockets in the search for more adequate understanding of human relationships.[2]

Psychologists speak about human relationships. Pastoral theologians speak about "loving one another." The American Heritage Dictionary distinguishes between love as "a deep, tender, ineffable feeling of affection and solicitude toward a person," and a theological virtue defined in Christianity as "love directed first toward God but also oneself and one's neighbors as objects of God's love."[3]

Interestingly, "(loving) oneself" is included in the dictionary definition of love as a theological virtue. Psychologists and theologians alike would surely agree that a healthy regard or love of oneself is a precondition for the ability to love others. Is there a clue here to where things have gone wrong in a world in which there is so much inability to love others, so much enmity and killing? What might that say about where teaching and education should begin?

Opening Prayer

> Oh the happiness of the heavenly Alleluia,
> sung in security, in no fear of adversity!
> We shall have no enemies in heaven, we
> shall never lose a friend. God's praises are
> sung both there and here. Here they are
> sung in hope, there, in hope's fulfillment;
> here they are sung by wayfarers, there, by
> those living in their own country.[4]

RETREAT SESSION TWO

In the late '70s, while Nouwen was teaching at Yale, he befriended a journalist who had come to interview him for a magazine article. Nouwen sensed from the very onset of the interview that the journalist wasn't at all enjoying what he was doing, and confronted him with this. Fred, the journalist, admitted he found his work boring. Nouwen, probing deeper, found that what the journalist really wanted to do was write a novel. Typically, Nouwen told Fred to quit his job and come to Yale as a scholar in residence. He, Nouwen, would find a way to provide the money.

At first Fred was uneasy and suspicious of the motivation that might be behind such a generous offer, but, eventually, convinced of Nouwen's integrity, he accepted the offer, and took up residence at Yale. It was the beginning of a friendship that would flower and last until Nouwen's death some twenty years later. The novel was never written, but as a result of the friendship a book was written by Nouwen at Fred's request.

Over the years he was Nouwen's friend, Fred Bratman read Henri's books and admired his engaging style. But as a self-declared secular Jew, he could hardly assimilate, much less be converted to Nouwen's patently Christian convictions. One day, while walking the streets of New York with Henri, he said, "Why don't you write something about the spiritual life for me and my friends?... You have something to say," he continued, "but you keep saying it to people who least need to hear it.... What about us young, ambitious, secular men and women wondering what life is all about after all? Can you speak to us with the same conviction as you speak to those who share your tradition, your language and your vision?"[5]

Fred pressed on: "Speak to us about the deepest yearnings of our hearts, about our many wishes, about hope; not about the many strategies for survival, but about trust; not about new methods of satisfying our emotional needs, but about love. Speak to us about a vision larger than our changing perspectives and about a voice deeper than the clamorings of our mass media. Yes, speak to us about something or someone greater than ourselves. Speak to us about...God."

Nouwen protested, suggesting that he simply was not qualified to do what his friend was asking: "Who am I to speak about such things?... I don't have the experience, the knowledge or the language you are asking for. You and your friends live in a world so different from my own."

Fred would not be put off: "You can do it.... You have to do it.... Visit me more often; talk to my friends; look attentively at what you see, and listen carefully to what you hear. You will discover a cry welling up from the depths of the human heart that has remained unheard because there was no one to listen."[6]

Nouwen felt overwhelmed. "What could I possibly say to a world of rushing taxicabs, glass-covered office towers and show business going on day and night?"

Over Nouwen's continued objections, Fred pressed forward: "Speak from that place in your heart where you are most yourself. Speak directly, simply, lovingly, gently and without any apologies. Tell us what you see and want us to see; tell us what you hear and want us to hear.... Trust your own heart. The words will come. There is nothing to fear. Those who need you most will help you most. You can be sure that I will."[7]

Out of this lively exchange came a new book: *Life of the Beloved: Spiritual Living in a Secular World.* The book begins with Nouwen telling the story of how he met his friend Fred at Yale, and how it was at Fred's request that this book has been written. In fact the book is written as addressed personally to Fred. He explains in the Prologue:

> I have chosen to speak directly—as I would in a personal letter. By keeping Fred and his friends at the center of my attention, I can best express what is in my heart. I am not able to deal with all the burning issues of our time and society, but I am able to write to a dear friend whom I came to know and love as a fellow-traveler searching for life, light and truth. I hope that through my being so personal and direct many may want to "listen in" and even join in this spiritual search.[8]

Apparently, readers didn't seem to mind at all that the book was a personal letter to Fred. Since its publication in 1992, the book has sold over two hundred thousand copies.[9]

As the title suggests, the book has been built around a single major biblical theme, the story of the baptism of Jesus of Nazareth. Nouwen dismisses the possible objection that he is quoting a text from the Christian tradition to convince his friend who is a secular Jew, insisting: "Our many conversations led me to the inner conviction that the words, 'You are my Beloved' revealed the most intimate truth about all human beings, whether they belong to any particular tradition or not." He goes on:

> Fred, all I want to say to you is "You are the Beloved," and all I hope is that you can hear these words as spoken to you with all the tenderness and force that love can hold. My only desire is to make these words reverberate in every corner of your being—"You are the Beloved."[10]

Nouwen acknowledges that it is not easy to take these words personally. In fact he suggests that the problem of taking the words seriously and personally is not a denominational problem but a universal problem: "It certainly is not easy to hear that voice in a world filled with voices that shout: 'You are no good, you are ugly; you are worthless; you are despicable, you are nobody—unless you can demonstrate the opposite.'"[11]

He goes on to alert his friend to the trap of self-rejection:

> Over the years, I have come to realize that the greatest trap in our life is not success, popularity or power, but self-rejection. Success, popularity and power can, indeed, present a great temptation, but

their seductive quality often comes from the way they are part of the much larger temptation to self-rejection. When we have come to believe in the voices that call us worthless and unlovable, then success, popularity and power are easily perceived as attractive solutions. The real trap, however, is self-rejection.

Maybe you think that you are more tempted by arrogance than by self-rejection. But isn't arrogance, in fact, the other side of self-rejection? Isn't arrogance putting yourself on a pedestal to avoid being seen as you see yourself? Isn't arrogance, in the final analysis, just another way of dealing with the feelings of worthlessness? Both self-rejection and arrogance pull us out of the common reality of existence and make a gentle community of people extremely difficult, if not impossible, to attain. I know too well that beneath my arrogance there lies much self-doubt, just as there is a great amount of pride hidden in my self-rejection. Whether I am inflated or deflated, I lose touch with my truth and distort my vision of reality.

...Self-rejection is the greatest enemy of the spiritual life because it contradicts the sacred voice that calls us the "Beloved." Being the Beloved expresses the core truth of our existence.[12]

In illustrating the profound difference that self-perception can make, Nouwen offers a case history of sorts, profiling two men: one who could believe that he was loved and one who could not:

> Judas and Peter present me with the choice between running away from Jesus in despair or returning to him in hope. Judas betrayed Jesus and hanged himself. Peter denied Jesus and returned to him in tears.
>
> Sometimes despair seems an attractive choice, solving everything in the negative. The voice of despair says, "I sin over and over again. After endless promises to myself and others to do better next time, I find myself back again in the old dark places. Forget about trying to change. I have tried for years. It didn't work and it will never work. It is better that I get out of people's way, be forgotten, no longer around, dead."
>
> This strangely attractive voice takes all uncertainties away and puts an end to the struggle. It speaks unambiguously for the darkness and offers a clear-cut negative identity.
>
> But Jesus came to open my ears to another voice that says, "I am your God, I have molded you with my own hands, and I love what I have made. I love you with a love that has no limits, because I love you as I am loved. Do not run away from me. Come back to me—not once, not twice, but always again. You are my child. How can you ever doubt that I will embrace you again, hold you against my breast, kiss you and let my hands run

through your hair? I am your God—the
God of mercy and compassion, the God of
pardon and love, the God of tenderness
and care. Please do not say that I have
given up on you, that I cannot stand you
anymore, that there is no way back. It is
not true. I so much want you to be with
me. I so much want you to be close to me.
I know all your thoughts. I hear all your
words. I see all of your actions. And I love
you because you are beautiful, made in
my own image, an expression of my most
intimate love. Do not judge yourself. Do
not condemn yourself. Do not reject
yourself. Let my love touch the deepest,
most hidden corners of your heart and
reveal to you your own beauty, a beauty
that you have lost sight of, but which will
become visible to you again in the light of
my mercy. Come, come, let me wipe your
tears, and let my mouth come close to
your ear and say to you, 'I love you, I love
you, I love you.'"

This is the voice that Jesus wants us to
hear. It is the voice that calls us always to
return to the one who has created us in
love and wants to re-create us in mercy.
Peter heard that voice and trusted it. As
he let that voice touch his heart, tears
came—tears of sorrow and tears of joy,
tears of remorse and tears of peace, tears
of repentance and tears of gratitude.

It is not easy to let the voice of God's
mercy speak to us because it is a voice
asking for an always open relationship,

one in which sins are acknowledged, forgiveness received, and love renewed. It does not offer us a solution, but a friendship. It does not take away our problems, but promises not to avoid them. It does not tell us where it will end, but assures us that we will never be alone. A true relationship is hard work because loving is hard work, with many tears and many smiles. But it is God's work and worth every part of it.

O Lord, my Lord, help me to listen to your voice and choose your mercy.[13]

For Reflection

- *Ultimately, what shapes our lives are the voices to which we listen. In a highly technological society there are so many voices calling out to us. Make a list of the voices that compete daily for your attention: Advertising from all directions—newspapers, TV, radio, billboards, telemarketers, magazines, bumper stickers, the uninvited guests in your mailbox—and more voices: your friends, your family, your neighbors and coworkers and your own inner voice.*

- *Which of these voices most influence your thinking, which claim most of your time and attention? Is it time to cut back on some of the lesser voices so that more attention can be given to the more important voices? Perhaps you might cut back on subscriptions for which you pay but don't have time to use. Do you set apart enough time to listen to the voice of your spouse? Your children?*

■ *Set aside a half-hour to listen to the voice of God calling you Beloved. If this seems too hard, plan ahead to set aside at least ten or fifteen minutes, or whatever is possible in your situation. Listen attentively. Accept your belovedness. Do not fight it. If you find yourself resisting it, stop resisting and surrender. Allow yourself to be embraced and loved by God. Eventually you will want to continue this practice on a daily basis. When at last you can come to accepting your belovedness, ask yourself how this new understanding of yourself might influence how you relate to others who are also God's beloved ones.*

Closing Prayer

Dear Lord, I bring before you all the people who experience failure in their search for a creative, affectionate relationship. Many single people feel lonely and unable to sustain a friendship for a long period of time; many married people feel frustrated in their marriage and separate to go different ways; many children cannot speak to their parents; and many parents have become afraid of their children. All around me I see the hunger for love and the inability to experience it in a deep and lasting way.

O Lord, look with favor on us, your people, and impart your love to us—not as an idea or concept, but as a lived experience. We can only love each other because you have loved us first. Let us know that first love so that we can see all human love as a reflection of a greater love, a love without conditions and limitations.

Heal those who feel hurt in their most intimate self, who feel rejected, misunderstood or even misused. Show them your healing love and help them on the way to forgiveness and reconciliation. Amen.[14]

Notes

1. Thomas Merton, *Conjectures of a Guilty Bystander* (Garden City, N.J.: Doubleday, 1966).

2. Carl R. Rogers, *On Becoming a Person* (Boston: Houghton Mifflin, 1961), p. ix.

3. *American Heritage Dictionary* (Boston: Houghton Mifflin, 1961).

4. St. Augustine, *Sermon 256*

5. Henri Nouwen, *Life of the Beloved* (New York: Crossroad, 1992), pp. 16–17.

6. *Life of the Beloved*, pp. 18–19.

7. *Life of the Beloved*, p. 20.

8. *Life of the Beloved*, pp. 20–21.

9. Source for sales data: Catholic Book Publishers Association.

10. *Life of the Beloved*, p. 26.

11. *Life of the Beloved*, p. 26.

12. *Life of the Beloved*, pp. 27–28.

13. *Road to Daybreak, A Spiritual Journey* (New York: Doubleday Image Books, 1988), pp. 157–158.

14. *A Cry for Mercy*, p. 52.

DAY THREE

Human Experience and Scriptural Foundations

Men go abroad to wonder at the height of mountains, at the huge waves of the sea, at the long courses of the rivers, at the vast compass of the ocean, at the circular motion of the stars—yet they pass by themselves without wondering.
    —Saint Augustine[1]

Coming Together in the Spirit

Nouwen's emphasis on our identity as Beloved may sound to some a bit removed from the "real world." Hence it is important, I think, that we visit for a moment a scene from this "real world." For good measure let's visit the real world at its worst. Let's go back in time to revisit the death camps of World War II in Europe. Our guide will be Viktor Frankl as he reports the scene he witnessed as a prisoner in the concentration camp at Auschwitz in his book originally entitled *From Death Camp to Existentialism,* later published under the title *Man's Search for Meaning.*

Frankl, a Jewish psychiatrist, notes in his journal:

> We who lived in concentration camps can
> remember the men who walked through
> the huts comforting others, giving away
> their last piece of bread. They may have
> been few in number, but they offer
> sufficient proof that everything can be
> taken from a man but one thing: the last
> of the human freedoms—to choose one's
> attitude in any given set of circumstances,
> to choose one's own way.[2]
>
> Occasionally I looked at the sky,
> where the stars were fading and the pink
> light of the morning was beginning to
> spread behind a dark bank of clouds. But
> my mind clung to my wife's image,
> imagining it with an uncanny acuteness. I
> heard her answering me, saw her smile,
> her frank and encouraging look. Real or
> not, her look was then more luminous
> than the sun which was beginning to rise.
>
> ...In a position of utter desolation,
> when man cannot express himself in
> positive action, when his only
> achievement may consist in enduring his
> sufferings in the right way—an honorable
> way—in such a position man can, through
> loving contemplation of the image he
> carries of his beloved, achieve fulfillment.
> For the first time in my life I was able to
> understand the meaning of the words,
> "The angels are lost in perpetual
> contemplation of an infinite glory."[3]

Later, Frankl tells the story of a young woman in the camp:

> ...like the story of the young woman whose
> death I witnessed in a concentration camp.
> It is a simple story. There is little to tell and
> it may sound as if I had invented it; but to
> me it seems like a poem.
>
> This young woman knew that she
> would die in the next few days. But when
> I talked to her she was cheerful in spite of
> this knowledge. "I am grateful that fate
> has hit me so hard," she told me. "In my
> former life I was spoiled and did not take
> spiritual accomplishments seriously."
> Pointing through the window of the hut,
> she said, "This tree here is the only friend
> I have in my loneliness." Through that
> window she could see just one branch of a
> chestnut tree, and on the branch were two
> blossoms. "I often talk to this tree," she
> said to me. I was startled and didn't quite
> know how to take her words. Was she
> delirious? Did she have occasional
> hallucinations? Anxiously I asked her if
> the tree replied. "Yes." What did it say to
> her? She answered, "It said to me, 'I am
> here—I am here—I am life, eternal life.'"[4]

In Frankl's experience it seems that in the real world,
when all else is stripped away, there is one thing that
cannot be taken away: the flame of love that burns in
one's heart—both the love given, and the love received.
"The salvation of man is through love and in love."[5]
It is no mere romanticism that Nouwen offers his readers
but his own experience of having listened to and believed

the voice that called him Beloved, and how it transformed
his life.

Opening Prayer

> I love the Lord, for [the Lord] has heard
> The cry of my appeal.
> The Lord was attentive to me
> In the day when I called.
> They surrounded me, the snares of death,
> With the anguish of the tomb.
> They caught me, sorrow and distress.
> I called on the Lord's name.
> O Lord, my God, deliver me.
> I was helpless, so God saved me.[6]

RETREAT SESSION THREE

Let us revisit Nouwen's statement to his friend, Fred:
"Our many conversations led me to the inner conviction
that the words, 'You are my Beloved' revealed the most
intimate truth about all human beings, whether they
belong to any particular tradition or not."[7] One may not
agree with Nouwen, but there is no doubt regarding his
own belief nor that he was deeply influenced and
determined to live according to this belief for the rest of
his life.

The Gospel Texts

The narrative referring to the baptism of Jesus appears in all three synoptic Gospels, and is alluded to in the first chapter of John's Gospel, verses 32–34. These are the sources to which we must attend if we are to come to some understanding of our human connectedness with Jesus in his identity as the "Beloved." Let us begin by looking at the full text relating the baptism of Jesus as it appears in the Gospel of Mark, the text quoted by Nouwen: [8]

> In those days Jesus came from Nazareth of Galilee and was baptized by John in the Jordan. And just as he was coming up out of the water, he saw the heavens torn apart and the Spirit descending like a dove on him. And a voice came from heaven, "You are my Son, the Beloved; with you I am well pleased." (Mark 1:9–11)

Matthew's account is longer:

> Then Jesus came from Galilee to John at the Jordan, to be baptized by him. John would have prevented him, saying, "I need to be baptized by you, and do you come to me?" But Jesus answered him, "Let it be so now; for it is proper for us in this way to fulfill all righteousness." Then he consented. And when Jesus had been baptized, just as he came up from the water, suddenly the heavens were opened to him and he saw the Spirit of God descending like a dove and alighting on him. And a voice from heaven said, "This is my Son, the Beloved, with whom I am well pleased." (Matthew 3:13–17)

Luke's account is basically the same as Matthew's and Mark's, but with distinctive details of his own:

> Now when all the people were baptized,
> and when Jesus also had been baptized
> and was praying, the heaven was opened,
> and the Holy Spirit descended upon him
> in bodily form like a dove. And a voice
> came from heaven, "You are my Son, the
> Beloved; with you I am well pleased."
> (Luke 3:21–22)

John's Gospel presents John the Baptist remembering the baptism of Jesus as a past event:

> And John testified, "I saw the Spirit
> descending from heaven like a dove, and
> it remained on him. I myself did not know
> him, but the one who sent me to baptize
> with water said to me, 'He on whom you
> see the Spirit descend and remain is the
> one who baptizes with the Holy Spirit.'
> And I myself have seen and have testified
> that this is the Son of God." (John 1:32–34)

Let's remember now what Nouwen says to his friend, Fred, about these texts:

> For many years I had read these words
> and even reflected upon them in sermons
> and lectures, but it is only since our talks
> in New York that they have taken on a
> meaning far beyond the boundaries of my
> own tradition. *Our many conversations led*
> *me to the inner conviction that the words,*
> *"You are my Beloved" revealed the most*
> *intimate truth about all human beings,*
> *whether they belong to any particular*
> *tradition or not.*[9]

Nouwen's claim is a bold one, stunning, if one takes it
seriously, a claim that invites a response: either a yes or a
no from the reader. Could it be that he is right? If he is, it
is certainly good news for all of us. If he is mistaken, then
we must ask: What other explanation could there be for
God to become human in Jesus? Indirectly he seems to get
support from at least one significant source, Pope John
XXIII, who is quoted as saying on his deathbed:

> ...Those open arms (of the crucified Jesus)
> have been the program of my
> pontificate: they mean that Christ died for
> all, for all. No one is excluded
> from his love, from his forgiveness.[10]

Elaborating on Henri's understanding of Christ, Michael
O'Laughlin writes:

> See here is the problem: if my authentic
> spirituality is about me—and the gospel is
> about Jesus—then where is the
> connection? How can I live the gospels?
> We really have put Jesus on a pedestal.
> He's way up there, like the jet stream. Not
> really on our planet. How can I go from
> admiring and fearing Jesus as an abstract
> figure in a story to something more?
>   Henri found the answer to this
> question in the words spoken at Jesus'
> baptism: This is my beloved son, in whom
> I am well pleased. When Henri progressed
> through his long meditation on
> Rembrandt's famous painting of the
> Return of the Prodigal Son, he realized
> that these words are a blessing from the
> Father. Jesus is about to begin his ministry,
> and before he begins, God speaks to him

in front of everyone and says: You are my
Son. I love you and take delight in you.
Now go. This is how Jesus faces the
temptations of Satan in the desert and all
the tribulations that he will endure later.
He does not allow his own doubts and
fears and the world's rejection of him
triumph over the voice that blessed him.
He had God's blessing, and he held on to
it. *Hold on to the blessing.*

Slowly, hesitantly, Henri began to test
this idea—am I also God's beloved? Many
parts of the New Testament seem to say
so. Paul says we are co-heirs with Christ.
John says that Christ is a revelation of the
love of the Father, and that we are all his
children. In his writings and in his
prayers, Henri began to claim an ever-
greater overlap between his life and the
life of Jesus. He began to interpret the life
of Jesus as more than a story from the
past. Rather, he saw it as a blueprint for
spiritual living![11]

In an enigmatic but beautiful statement Saint Bernard of
Clairvaux may help us to navigate this profound mystery
of which Nouwen speaks—our connectedness to God
and God's connectedness to us in Jesus. He expresses it
this way:

In his first work he gave me myself, in his
second he gave himself, and by giving
himself he gave me back myself. Given,
therefore, and then given back, I owe
myself in return for myself, and I owe
myself twice. And yet, what could I give
to God for himself?[12]

We are not dealing with "proof texts" here. We are comparing the thoughts of two writers who probed deeply the mystery of the incarnation and its implications for us at the human level. Saint Bernard concluded: "...(God)...by giving himself...*gave me back myself.*" Nouwen says he was led to the inner conviction that "... the words, 'You are my Beloved' revealed the most intimate truth about all human beings, whether they belong to any particular tradition or not."

If this identification of Christ with all of humanity and all of humanity with Christ as "Beloved" sounds "too good to be true," too "easy" for the rest of us, it might be well to take a closer look at the texts that give the account of the baptism of Jesus. As a follow-up retreat exercise, write on a piece of paper the textual references in the four Gospels that refer to the narratives relating the story of the baptism of Jesus. In order they are as follows: Matthew 3:13–17; Mark 1:9–11; Luke 3:21–22; John 1:32–34. Read each of the accounts, then make note of the following: In all three of the synoptic Gospels the account of the baptism of Jesus is followed by the narrative relating the temptation of Jesus in the desert. Both Matthew's and Mark's accounts move swiftly from the baptism scene to the desert:

> And a voice from heaven said, "This is my Son, the Beloved, with whom I am well pleased." Then Jesus was led by the Spirit into the wilderness to be tempted by the devil. (Matthew 3:17–4:1)

> And a voice came from heaven, "You are my the Son, the Beloved; with you I am well pleased." And the Spirit immediately drove him out into the wilderness. He was in the wilderness forty days, tempted by

Satan; and he was with the wild beasts;
and the angels waited on him. (Mark
1:11–12)

The election and mission of Jesus is not presented in terms
of an all-expenses-paid trip to a heavenly Las Vegas. Jesus
is planted squarely in the center of the world in which we
live, complete with the allurements and deceptions we all
eventually face. Nouwen does not soft peddle this aspect
of our "Belovedness." He walks us through it.

Speaking to his friend Fred, Nouwen goes on to
develop his point:

> From the moment we claim the truth of
> being the Beloved, we are faced with the
> call to become who we are. Becoming the
> Beloved is the great spiritual journey we
> have to make.... *Becoming the Beloved means
> letting the truth of our Belovedness become
> enfleshed in everything we think, say or do....*
> Becoming the Beloved is pulling the truth
> revealed to me from above down into the
> ordinariness of what I am, in fact,
> thinking of, talking about and doing from
> hour to hour.[13]

For Reflection:

■ *Viktor Frankl, speaking of his experience in concentration
camps in the opening pages of this day's retreat, states:
"...everything can be taken from a man but one thing: the
last of the human freedoms—to choose one's attitude in
any given set of circumstances, to choose one's own way."
Think back on some of your own past unpleasant or
painful experiences. Can you remember an instance when
you exercised that "last" freedom of which Frankl speaks?*

- *Think ahead of a recurring difficulty you must face daily or frequently at home or in the workplace, whether it be a person or some other trying demand on your patience or energy. Then choose your attitude—in advance.*

- *Frankl also notes the story of the woman dying in the concentration camp, but found looking through her window at a single branch of a chestnut tree with two blossoms, a symbol of eternal life. How often do you commune with nature to help you deepen your perceptions of the daily miracles that surround you? Walking is good for the soul as well as for the body. Find a friendly place for walking and bless it with your regular visits.*

- *Reflect prayerfully on the Gospel accounts of the baptism of Jesus, putting yourself in the place of Jesus. Be sure to include the Gospel passages that follow, giving the account of the temptations of Jesus in the desert. In what way can you identify with those temptations in your own life?*

- *Write in your personal journal the entire text of the words of Saint Bernard quoted above: "...by giving himself he gave me back myself...." Make a point of revisiting and assimilating them frequently.*

Closing Prayer

O Lord, you have searched me and
known me
You know when I sit down and when I
rise up,
you discern my thoughts from far away.
You search out my path and my lying
down,
And are acquainted with all my ways.

For it was you who formed my inward
parts;
You knit me together in my mother's
womb.
I praise you, for I am fearfully and
wonderfully made.
(Psalm 139:1–3, 13–14).[14]

Notes

1. Quoted in Paul Thigpen, *A Dictionary of Quotes from the Saints* (Ann Arbor, Mich.: Servant Publications, 2001), p. 119.

2. Viktor Frankl, *Man's Search for Meaning.* Original Title: *From Death Camp to Existentialism.* "Book of the Year" in 1961–62 by Colby College Copyright: Washington Square Press, 1959, 1963, Distributed by Simon & Schuster. (Boston: Beacon Press, 1959), p. 104.

3. Frankl, pp. 36–37.

4. Frankl, pp. 68–69.

5. Frankl, p. 36.

6. Psalm 16:1–4, 6. Grail Translation.

7. *Life of the Beloved,* p. 26.

8. *Life of the Beloved,* p. 26.

9. *Life of the Beloved,* p. 26.

10. Thomas Cahill, Pope John XXIII (New York: Viking Penguin, 2002), "The Three Secrets of John XXIII."

11. When I passed the first draft of this retreat around to selected readers for their comments or suggestions, it was precisely this section that drew a pointed response from my friend, Michael O'Laughlin. Michael wrote in the margin: "Expand this central idea of Henri's—explain its origin and novelty." I wrote back to

Michael: "What precisely is its origin? Where did Henri get this deep conviction?" My question thrown back to Michael led him to writing a whole paper to which he gave the title: "Henri's Christ." This section is a quote from his paper. Michael O'Laughlin currently works as a spiritual director at the healing center in Arlington, Massachusetts. His latest book project is *Jesus: A Gospel*, by Henri Nouwen, edited with an introduction by Michael O'Laughlin (Maryknoll, N.Y.: Orbis, 2001). He was assistant teacher to Henri Nouwen at Harvard in the spring of 1983 and 1984.

12. *Charles Dumont, Pathway of Peace: Cistercian Wisdom According to St. Bernard,* Elizabeth Connor O.S.C.O., trans. (Kalamazoo, Mich.: Cistercian Publications, 1999), pp. 76–77.

13. *Life of the Beloved,* pp. 37, 39, emphasis added.

14. Psalm 139.

DAY FOUR
Becoming the Beloved

When he had spent everything, a severe famine took place throughout that country, and he began to be in need. So he went and hired himself out to one of the citizens of that country, who sent him to his fields to feed the pigs. He would gladly have filled himself with the pods that the pigs were eating; and no one gave him anything But when he came to himself he said, "How many of my father's hired hands have bread enough and to spare, but here I am dying of hunger! I will get up and go to my father...". [W]hile he was still far off, his father saw him and was filled with compassion; he ran and put his arms around him and kissed him.... [T]he father said to his slaves, "Quickly, bring out a robe-the best one-and put it on him; put a ring on his finger and sandals on his feet...and let us eat and celebrate; for this son of mine was dead and is alive again; he was lost and is found!"

Coming Together in the Spirit

There is yet one more gem to be mined from the wisdom of the concentration camp, as related by Viktor Frankl. He relates the complaints he heard regularly from the crushed spirits of the men in the camp with him and how he dealt with them. More than once he heard the despairing voice that declared with finality: "I have nothing to expect from life anymore."

Reflecting on these words, Frankl mused:

> What sort of answer can one give to that? What was really needed was a fundamental change in our attitude toward life. We had to learn ourselves and, furthermore, we had to teach the despairing men, that it did not really matter what we expected from life, but rather what life expected from us. We needed to stop asking about the meaning of life, and instead to think of ourselves as those who were being questioned by life— daily and hourly.... Life ultimately means taking the responsibility to find the right answer to its problems and to fulfill the tasks which it constantly sets for each individual.[2]

In seeking to reclaim our humanity, we have been led by Henri Nouwen to listen to the voice that calls us Beloved. He tells his readers—in the person of his friend, Fred— that once "we claim the truth of being the Beloved, we are faced with the call to become who we are.... Becoming the Beloved means letting the truth of our Belovedness become enfleshed in everything we think, say or do."[3]

How does one go about living out this Belovedness? Nouwen proposes a discipline derived from four words, suggested to him by his daily celebration of the Eucharist: "taken, blessed, broken and given." It will be the task of the fourth and fifth days of our retreat to explore with our retreat director the disciplines to which these four words invite us, enabling us to become who we are.

Opening Prayer

> Make me to know your ways, O Lord
>   teach me your paths.
> Lead me in your truth, and teach me
>   for you are the God of my
>   salvation;
>   for you I wait all day long.
> (Psalm 25:4–5)

Retreat Session Four

Taken and Blessed

Commenting on the first word, "taken," Nouwen suggests that another warmer, softer word with basically the same meaning should take its place, a word with a rich biblical background: *"chosen."* Speaking to his Jewish friend Fred, Nouwen acknowledges that the word has both positive and negative associations: the honor of being God's "chosen people," but also a history of being a people singled out for persecution. With that understood, Nouwen goes on to explain why "chosen," in the sense he intends it, is a key word that sheds light on our relationship to God as Beloved.

In a competitive world, being chosen often means someone gets rejected. For one sports team to win, another has to lose. Nouwen gives the sad example of the mother who says to her child: "I hadn't really expected you, but once I found out that I was pregnant I decided to have you anyway.... You were sort of an accident." This does not enhance a person's self-image. He distinguishes this kind of chosenness from what it means to be chosen by God:

> Long before any human being saw us, we
> are seen by God's loving eyes. Long
> before anyone heard us cry or laugh, we
> are heard by our God who is all ears for
> us. Long before any person spoke to us in
> this world, we are spoken to by the voice
> of eternal love. Our preciousness,
> uniqueness and individuality are not
> given to us by those who meet us in clock-
> time—our brief chronological existence—
> but by the One who has chosen us with an
> everlasting love, a love that existed from
> all eternity and will last through all
> eternity.[4]

Nouwen next poses the question: "How do we get in
touch with our chosenness when we are surrounded by
rejections?" He offers three guidelines:

> First of all, you have to keep unmasking
> the world about you for what it is:
> manipulative, controlling, power-hungry
> and, in the long run, destructive. The
> world tells you many lies about who you
> are, and you simply have to be realistic
> enough to remind yourself of this. Every
> time you feel hurt, offended or rejected,
> you have to dare to say to yourself:
> "These feelings, strong as they may be, are
> not telling me the truth about myself. The
> truth, even though I cannot feel it right
> now, is that I am the chosen child of God,
> precious in God's eyes, called the Beloved
> from all eternity and held safe in an
> everlasting embrace."

Secondly, you have to keep looking for
people and places where your truth is
spoken and where you are reminded of
your deepest identity as the chosen one.
Yes, we must dare to opt consciously for
our chosenness and not allow our
emotions, feelings or passions to seduce
us into self-rejection.[5]

Nouwen strongly recommends that we keep in touch with
our local churches, synagogues and faith communities and
support groups, and with our family and friends who can
keep reminding us of the truth of who we are: precious in
God's eyes.

"Thirdly," he insists, "you have to celebrate
your chosenness constantly":

This means saying "thank you" to God for
having chosen you, and "thank you" to all
who remind you of your chosenness.
Gratitude is the most fruitful way of
deepening your consciousness that you
are not an "accident," but a divine choice.[6]

Recognizing that none of us is good at being faithful to
our best intentions and resolutions, Nouwen goads us on
and warns us not to be discouraged by our failures:

Before I know it, I find myself
complaining again, brooding again about
some rejection and plotting ways to take
revenge, but when I keep my disciplines
close to my heart, I am able to step over
my shadow into the light of my truth.[7]

Notably, he concludes:

When we claim and constantly reclaim the
truth of being the chosen ones, we soon

discover within ourselves a deep desire to reveal to others their own chosenness. Instead of making us feel that we are better, more precious or valuable than others, our awareness of being chosen opens our eyes to the chosenness of others. That is the great joy of being chosen: the discovery that others are chosen as well. In the house of God there are many mansions. There is a place for everyone—a unique, special place. Once we deeply trust that we ourselves are precious in God's eyes, we are able to recognize the preciousness of others and their unique places in God's heart.[8]

As God's Beloved and chosen ones we are blessed. Nouwen explains what it means to be blessed:

I am increasingly aware of how much we fearful, anxious, insecure human beings are in need of a blessing. Children need to be blessed by their parents and parents by their children. We all need each other's blessings—masters and disciple, rabbis and students, bishops and priests, doctors and patients.

Let me first tell you what I mean by the word "blessing." In Latin, to bless is *benedicere*. The word "benediction" that is used in many churches means literally: speaking (*dictio*) well (*bene*) or saying good things of someone. That speaks to me. I need to hear good things said of me, and I know how much you have the same need. Nowadays, we often say: "We have

to affirm each other." Without affirmation,
it is hard to live well. *To give someone a
blessing is the most significant affirmation we
can offer.* It is more than a word of praise
or appreciation; it is more than pointing
out someone's talents or good deeds; it is
more than putting someone in the light.
To give a blessing is to affirm, to say "yes"
to a person's Belovedness. And more than
that: to give a blessing creates the reality
of which it speaks. There is a lot of mutual
admiration in this world, just as there is a
lot of mutual condemnation. A blessing
goes beyond the distinction between
admiration or condemnation, between
virtues or vices, between good deeds or
evil deeds. A blessing touches the original
goodness of the other and calls forth his
or her Belovedness.

Not long ago, in my own community,
I had a very personal experience of the
power of a real blessing. Shortly before I
started a prayer service in one of our
houses, Janet, a handicapped member of
our community, said to me: "Henri, can
you give me a blessing?" I responded in a
somewhat automatic way by tracing with
my thumb the sign of the cross on her
forehead. Instead of being grateful,
however, she protested vehemently, "No,
that doesn't work. I want a real blessing!"
I suddenly became aware of the ritualistic
quality of my response to her request and
said, "Oh, I am sorry,...let me give you a
real blessing when we are all together for

the prayer service." She nodded with a smile, and I realized that something special was required of me. After the service, when about thirty people were sitting in a circle on the floor, I said, "Janet has asked me for a special blessing. She feels that she needs that now." As I was saying this, I didn't know what Janet really wanted. But Janet didn't leave me in doubt for very long. As soon as I had said, "Janet has asked me for a special blessing," she stood up and walked toward me. I was wearing a long white robe with ample sleeves covering my hands as well as my arms. Spontaneously, Janet put her arms around me and put her head against my chest. Without thinking, I covered her with my sleeves so that she almost vanished in the folds of my robe. As we held each other, I said, "Janet, I want you to know that you are God's Beloved Daughter. You are precious in God's eyes. Your beautiful smile, your kindness to the people in your house and all the good things you do show us what a beautiful human being you are. I know you feel a little low these days and that there is some sadness in your heart, but I want you to remember who you are: a very special person, deeply loved by God and all the people who are here with you."

As I said these words, Janet raised her head and looked at me; and her broad smile showed that she had really heard and received the blessing. When she returned to her place, Jane, another handicapped woman, raised her hand and said, "I want a blessing too." She stood up and, before I knew it, had put her face against my chest. After I had spoken words of blessing to her, many more of the handicapped people followed, expressing the same desire to be blessed. The most touching moment, however, came when one of the assistants, a twenty-four-year-old student, raised his hand and said, "And what about me?" "Sure," I said, "Come." He came, and, as we stood before each other, I put my arms around him and said, "John, it is so good that you are here. You are God's Beloved Son. Your presence is a joy for all of us. When things are hard and life is burdensome, always remember that you are loved with an everlasting love." As I spoke these words, he looked at me with tears in his eyes and then he said, "Thank you, thank you very much."

That evening I recognized the importance of blessing and being blessed and reclaimed it as a true sign of the Beloved. The blessings that we give to each other are expressions of the blessing that rests on us from all eternity. It is the deepest affirmation of our true self. It is not enough to be chosen. We also need an ongoing blessing that allows us to hear in an ever-new way that we belong to a loving God who will never leave us alone, but will remind us always that

we are guided by love on every step of
our lives.[9]

Claiming our blessedness does not come easily in the
midst of daily struggles with our relationships, our work
and the many pressures that can come to bear on our
lives. Nouwen suggests two disciplines for claiming our
blessedness: the discipline of prayer and the cultivation of
presence:

> For me personally, prayer becomes more
> and more a way to listen to the blessing. I
> have read and written much about prayer,
> but when I go to a quiet place to pray, I
> realize that, although I have a tendency to
> say many things to God, the real "work"
> of prayer is to become silent and listen to
> the voice that says good things about me.
> This might sound self-indulgent, but, in
> practice, it is a hard discipline. I am so
> afraid of being cursed, of hearing that I
> am no good or not good enough, that I
> quickly give in to the temptation to start
> talking and to keep talking in order to
> control my fears. To gently push aside
> and silence the many voices that question
> my goodness and to trust that I will hear
> a voice of blessing...that demands real
> effort.
>
> Have you ever tried to spend a whole
> hour doing nothing but listening to the
> voice that dwells deep in your heart?
> When there is no radio to listen to, no TV
> to watch, no book to read, no person to
> talk to, no project to finish, no phone call
> to make, how does that make you feel?
> Often it does no more than make us so

aware of how much there is still to do that
we haven't yet done that we decide to
leave the fearful silence and go back to
work! It is not easy to enter into the
silence and reach beyond the many
boisterous and demanding voices of our
world and to discover there the small
intimate voice saying: "You are my
Beloved Child, on you my favor rests."
Still, if we dare to embrace our solitude
and befriend our silence, we will come to
know that voice. I do not want to suggest
to you that one day you will hear that
voice with your bodily ears. I am not
speaking about a hallucinatory voice, but
about a voice that can be heard by the ear
of faith, the ear of the inner heart. [10]

The faithful discipline of prayer reveals to
you that you are the blessed one and gives
you the power to bless others.[11]

By presence I mean attentiveness to the
blessings that come to you day after day,
year after year. The problem of modern
living is that we are too busy—looking for
affirmation in the wrong places?—to
notice that we are being blessed…. It has
become extremely difficult for us to stop,
listen, pay attention and receive gracefully
what is offered to us.[12]

This attentive presence can allow us to see
how many blessings there are for us to
receive: the blessings of the poor who stop
us on the road, the blessings of the
blossoming trees and fresh flowers that

tell us about new life, the blessings of music, painting, sculpture and architecture—all of that—but most of all the blessings that come to us through words of gratitude, encouragement, affection and love. These many blessings do not have to be invented. They are there, surrounding us on all sides. But we have to be present to them and receive them. They don't force themselves on us. They are gentle reminders of that beautiful, strong, but hidden, voice of the one who calls us by name and speaks good things about us.[13]

[C]laiming your own blessedness always leads to a deep desire to bless others. The characteristic of the blessed ones is that, wherever they go, they always speak words of blessing. It is remarkable how easy it is to bless others, to speak good things to and about them, to call forth their beauty and truth, when you yourself are in touch with your own blessedness. The blessed one always blesses. And people want to be blessed!... No one is brought to life through curses, gossip, accusations or blaming. There is so much of that taking place around us all the time. And it calls forth only darkness, destruction and death. As the "blessed ones," we can walk through this world and offer blessings. It doesn't require much effort. It flows naturally from our hearts. When we hear within ourselves the voice calling us by name and blessing

us, the darkness no longer distracts us.
The voice that calls us the Beloved will
give us words to bless others and reveal
to them that they are no less blessed
than we.[14]

For Reflection

- Nouwen offers three guidelines to help us get in touch with our unique status as "chosen." The first is to "keep unmasking the world about you for what it is: manipulative, controlling, power-hungry...destructive." Read or watch the daily news and see how much unmasking you can do.

- In the same vein Nouwen says, "The world tells you many lies about who you are, and you simply have to be realistic enough to remind yourself of this." What lies has the world told you about who you are? How have you responded?

- Reflect with gratitude on the people in your life who have told you the truth about yourself, especially those who have encouraged you and influenced your long-term life decisions. You might want to send one of them a thank-you note.

- Nouwen suggests that we bless one another. If you are parents, make it a regular family practice to bless each of your children by a laying on of hands, or perhaps better, like Nouwen, with a big hug, holding them close to your heart, saying good things about them and lifting them up to God.

- Never lose an opportunity to bless others by saying good things about them and invoking God's blessing on them. Blessings are powerful words.

Closing Prayer

Page through the Book of Psalms and find your own closing prayer, looking for verses that speak of blessing(s). Spend time with those that appeal to you in a special way. Be sure to probe more than one version of the Psalms. For starters, you might want to begin with Psalms 103 and 104. Find a blessing that is particularly meaningful to you personally.

Notes

1. Luke 15:14–17, 22–24.

2. Frankl, pp. 76–77.

3. *Life of the Beloved*, pp. 37–39.

4. *Life of the Beloved*, pp. 48–49.

5. *Life of the Beloved*, pp. 49–50.

6. *Life of the Beloved*, p. 50.

7. *Life of the Beloved*, p. 52.

8. *Life of the Beloved*, pp. 52–53.

9. *Life of the Beloved*, pp. 56–59.

10. *Life of the Beloved*, pp. 62–63.

11. *Life of the Beloved*, p. 63.

12. *Life of the Beloved*, pp. 64–65.

13. *Life of the Beloved*, p. 66.

14. *Life of the Beloved*, p. 67.

DAY FIVE
Broken and Given

"It did not matter what we expected from life, but rather what life expected from us."
—Viktor Frankl[1]

Coming Together in the Spirit

I was seated on a flight from Seattle to Detroit, on my way home from a tour of Alaska, ten days after September 11. I had slipped into my carry-on a copy of Beldan Lane's book, *The Solace of Fierce Landscapes*. Still reeling from the unfolding reports of the fateful days past, my eyes fastened on these words in Lane's book: "In the beginning you weep. The starting point for many things is grief, at the place where endings seem so absolute. One would think it should be otherwise, but the pain of closing is antecedent to every new opening in our lives."[2]

With these words, born of his grief in watching his mother slowly wither away in a hospital bed, a victim of Alzheimer's, Lane redefined for me the meaning of the losses in my life and brought me to a deeper understanding of Nouwen's teaching on the life of the Beloved: "The leaders and prophets of Israel, who were clearly chosen and blessed, all lived very broken lives.

And we, the Beloved Sons and Daughters of God, cannot escape our brokenness either."[3]

If there is anything that powers the driving force of technology, it is the striving for radical change: to do things better, faster, at lower cost, to pave the way to a Utopia never before imagined. Nothing is more intolerable in moving toward this end than sand or grit in the wheels. Of no use whatever are broken wheels. Though Nouwen makes no reference to technology as such in the section to follow, his remarks on the constant of brokenness in the human condition stand in stark contrast to the models set before us by technology. They require us to make a U-turn in our thinking.

Opening Prayer

Dear Lord, you say, "Shoulder my yoke and learn from me, for I am gentle and humble in heart." These words stayed with me today because I realized how often I complain about my yoke and hear others complain about theirs. So often I consider life and its many tasks and concerns burdensome, and then it does not take much to become pessimistic or depressed, to ask for attention to my "unique" problems, and to spend much time and energy in expressing annoyance and irritation.

You do not say, "I will take your burden away," but, "I invite you to take on my burden!" Your burden is a real burden. It is the burden of all human sin and failings. You carried that burden and died under its weight. Thus you made it into a light burden.

O Lord, turn my attention from the
false burden to the real burden, and let me
carry your burden in union with you. I
know that only then will I be able to
overcome the temptations of bitterness
and resentfulness, and live joyfully and
gratefully in your service. Let me better
understand your words, "My yoke is easy
and my burden light." Amen. [4]

RETREAT SESSION FIVE

Broken

The first response...to our brokenness is to
face it squarely and befriend it. This may
seem quite unnatural. Our first, most
spontaneous response to pain and
suffering is to avoid it, to keep it at arm's
length; to ignore, circumvent or deny it.
Suffering—be it physical, mental or
emotional—is almost always experienced
as an unwelcome intrusion into our lives,
something that should not be there. It is
difficult, if not impossible, to see anything
positive in suffering; it must be avoided
away at all costs.

When this is, indeed, our spontaneous
attitude toward our brokenness, it is no
surprise that befriending it seems, at first,
masochistic. Still, my own pain in life has
taught me that the first step to healing is
not a step away from the pain, but a step
toward it. When brokenness is, in fact, just

as intimate a part of our being as our chosenness and our blessedness, we have to dare to overcome our fear and become familiar with it. Yes, we have to find the courage to embrace our own brokenness, to make our most feared enemy into a friend and to claim it as an intimate companion. I am convinced that healing is often so difficult because we don't want to know the pain.[5]

The deep truth is that our human suffering need not be an obstacle to the joy and peace we so desire, but can become, instead, the means *to* it. The great secret of the spiritual life, the life of the Beloved Sons and Daughters of God, is that everything we live, be it gladness or sadness, joy or pain, health or illness, can all be part of the journey toward the full realization of our humanity. It is not hard to say to one another: "All that is good and beautiful leads us to the glory of the children of God." But it is very hard to say: "But didn't you know that we all have to suffer and thus enter into our glory?" Nonetheless, real care means the willingness to help each other in making our brokenness into the gateway to joy.

The second response to our brokenness is to put it under the blessing. For me, this "putting of our brokenness under the blessing" is a precondition for befriending it. Our brokenness is often so frightening to face because we live it under the curse. Living our brokenness under the curse

means that we experience our pain as a
confirmation of our negative feelings
about ourselves. It is like saying, "I
always suspected that I was useless or
worthless, and now I am sure of it because
of what is happening to me." There is
always something in us searching for an
explanation of what takes place in our
lives and, if we have already yielded to
the temptation to self-rejection, then every
form of misfortune only deepens it. When
we lose a family member or friend
through death, when we become jobless,
when we fail an examination, when we
live through a separation or a divorce...the
question "Why?" spontaneously emerges.
"Why me?" "Why now?" "Why here?" It
is so arduous to live without an answer to
this "Why?" that we are easily seduced
into connecting the events over which we
have no control with our conscious or
unconscious evaluation.... Before we fully
realize it, we have already said to
ourselves: "You see, I always thought I
was no good.... Now I know for sure. The
facts of life prove it."

The great spiritual call of the Beloved
Children of God is to pull their brokenness
away from the shadow of the curse and
put it under the light of the blessing. This
is not as easy as it sounds. The powers of
the darkness around us are strong, and
our world finds it easier to manipulate
self-rejecting people than self-accepting
people. But when we keep listening

attentively to the voice calling us the
Beloved, it becomes possible to live our
brokenness, not as a confirmation of our
fear that we are worthless, but as an
opportunity to purify and deepen the
blessing that rests upon us. Physical,
mental or emotional pain lived under the
blessing is experienced in ways radically
different from physical, mental or
emotional pain lived under the curse.
Even a small burden, perceived as a sign
of our worthlessness, can lead us to deep
depression—even suicide. However, great
and heavy burdens become light and easy
when they are lived in the light of the
blessing. What seemed intolerable
becomes a challenge. What seemed a
reason for depression becomes a source of
purification. What seemed punishment
becomes a gentle pruning. What seemed
rejection becomes a way to a deeper
communion.

And so the great task becomes that of
allowing the blessing to touch us in our
brokenness. Then our brokenness will
gradually come to be seen as an opening
toward the full acceptance of ourselves as
the Beloved. This explains why true joy
can be experienced in the midst of great
suffering. It is the joy of being disciplined,
purified and pruned. Just as athletes who
experience great pain as they run the race
can, at the same time, taste the joy of
knowing that they are coming closer to
their goal, so also can the Beloved
experience suffering as a way to the

deeper communion for which they yearn. Here joy and sorrow are no longer each other's opposites, but have become the two sides of the same desire to grow to the fullness of the Beloved.[6]

We are chosen, blessed and broken so as to be given. The fourth aspect of the life of the Beloved is to be given. For me, personally, this means that it is only as people who are given that we can fully understand our being chosen, blessed and broken. In the giving it becomes clear that we are chosen, blessed and broken not simply for our own sakes, but so that all we live finds its final significance in its being lived for others.

...What a wonderful mystery this is! Our greatest fulfillment lies in giving ourselves to others. Although it often seems that people give only to receive, I believe that, beyond all our desires to be appreciated, rewarded and acknowledged, there lies a simple and pure desire to give. I remember how I once spent long hours looking in Dutch stores for a birthday gift for my father or mother, simply enjoying being able to give. Our humanity comes to its fullest bloom in giving.[7]

It is sad to see that, in our highly competitive and greedy world, we have lost touch with the joy of giving. We often live as if our happiness depended on having. But I don't know anyone who is really happy because of what he or she has. True joy, happiness and inner peace come from the giving of ourselves to others. A happy life is a life for others. That truth, however, is usually discovered when we are confronted with our brokenness.[8]

When we eat together we are vulnerable to one another. Around the table we can't wear weapons of any sort. Eating from the same bread and drinking from the same cup call us to live in unity and peace. This becomes very visible when there is a conflict. Then, eating and drinking together can become a truly threatening event, then the meal can become the most dreaded moment of the day. We all know about painful silences during dinner. They contrast starkly with the intimacy of eating and drinking together, and the distance between those sitting around the table can be unbearable.[9]

On the other hand, a really peaceful and joyful meal together belongs to the greatest moments of life.

Don't you think that our desire to eat together is an expression of our even deeper desire to be food for one another? Don't we sometimes say: "That was a very nurturing conversation. That was a refreshing time"? I think that our deepest human desire is to give ourselves to each other as a source of physical, emotional and spiritual growth. Isn't the baby at its mother's breast one of the most moving signs of human love? Isn't "tasting" the best word to express the experience of intimacy? Don't lovers in their ecstatic moments experience their love as a desire to eat and drink each other? As the Beloved ones, our greatest fulfillment lies in becoming bread for the world. That is the most intimate expression of our deepest desire to give ourselves to each other.[10]

Just as bread needs to be broken in order to be given, so, too, do our lives.[11]

As I grow older, I discover more and more that the greatest gift I have to offer is my own joy of living, my own inner peace, my own silence and solitude, my own sense of well-being. When I ask myself, "Who helps me most?" I must answer, "The one who is willing to share his or her life with me."

It is worthwhile making a distinction between talents and gifts. More important than our talents are our gifts. We may have only a few talents, but we have many gifts. Our gifts are the many ways in which we express our humanity. They are part of who we are: friendship, kindness, patience, joy, peace, forgiveness, gentleness, love, hope, trust and many others. These are the gifts we have to offer to each other.

...Secondly, we are called to give ourselves, not only in life, but in death as well. As the Beloved Children of God , we are called to make our death the greatest gift. Since it is true that we are broken so as to be given, then our final brokenness,

death, is to become the means to our final
gift of self. How can that be true? It seems
that death is the great enemy to be evaded
for as long as possible. Dying is not
something we like to think about or talk
about. Still, one of the very few things we
can be sure of is that we will die. I am
constantly amazed by the lengths to which
our society goes to prevent us from
preparing ourselves well for death.

For the Beloved Sons and Daughters of
God, dying is the gateway to the complete
experience of being the Beloved. For those
who know they are chosen, blessed and
broken to be given, dying is the way to
becoming pure gift.... How is this
possible?[12]

The fruitfulness of our little life, once we
recognize it and live it as the life of the
Beloved, is beyond anything we ourselves
can imagine. One of the greatest acts of
faith is to believe that the few years we live
on this earth are like a little seed planted in
a very rich soil. For this seed to bear fruit,
it must die. We often see or feel only the
dying, but the harvest will be abundant
even when we ourselves are not the
harvesters.

How different would our life be were
we truly able to trust that it multiplied in
being given away![13]

Imagine that, in the center of your heart,
you trust that your smiles and handshakes,
your embraces and your kisses are only the

early signs of a worldwide community of love and peace! Imagine that your trusting that every little movement of love you make will ripple out into ever new and wider circles—just as a little stone thrown into a still pond. Imagine, imagine.... Could you ever be depressed, angry, resentful or vengeful? Could you ever hate, destroy or kill? Could you ever despair of the meaning of your short earthly existence?[14]

The death of the Beloved bears fruit in many lives. You and I have to trust that our short little lives can bear fruit far beyond the boundaries of our chronologies. But we have to choose this and trust deeply that we have a spirit to send that will bring joy, peace and life to those who will remember us. Francis of Assisi died in 1226, but he is still very much alive! His death was a true gift, and today, nearly eight centuries later, he continues to fill his brothers and sisters, within and without the Franciscan Orders, with great energy and life. He died, but never died. His life goes on bearing new fruit around the world. His spirit keeps descending upon us. More than ever I am convinced that death can, indeed, be chosen as our final gift of life.[15]

For Reflection

- *Read or review the story of Franciscan priest Father Maximilian Kolbe, whose life was literally broken and given in the concentration camp of Auschwitz, when he volunteered to take the place of a married man, who was singled out to be sent to the starvation bunker for certain death.*[16]

■ *Reflect on the times you have suffered losses or been "broken." In retrospect can you find in any of these instances that they were prelude to a new beginning?*

■ *Reflect on the times you have been "given": in friendship, in marriage, in the workplace, in commitment to special causes to which you are dedicated. See them now in the context of the Eucharist, as Nouwen suggests.*

Closing Prayer

Blessed are You, O Radiant One,
You, who are hidden within
our hearts,
even as we are hidden within
your Heart!
...Open us that we might recognize the
divine in every person,
and become sensitive to all we
meet along the path.
For You are the Breathing Life of all,
the infinite and eternal within
our hearts.[17]

Notes

1. Frankl, p. 122

2. Beldan C. Lane, *The Solace of Fierce Landscapes: Exploring Desert and Mountain Spirituality* (New York: Oxford University Press, 1998).

3. *Life of the Beloved*, p. 70.

4. *A Cry For Mercy: Prayers From the Genesee*, p. 88.

5. *Life of the Beloved*, pp. 75–76.

6. *Life of the Beloved*, pp. 77–80.

7. *Life of the Beloved*, pp. 84–85.

8. *Life of the Beloved*, p. 87.

9. *Life of the Beloved*, pp. 88–89, emphasis added.

10. *Life of the Beloved*, p. 89.

11. *Life of the Beloved*, p. 88.

12. *Life of the Beloved*, pp. 90-93.

13. *Life of the Beloved*, pp. 98–99.

14. *Life of the Beloved*, pp. 98–99.

15. *Life of the Beloved*, pp. 96–97.

16. Antonio Ricciardi, O.F.M. Conv., trans., *St. Maximilian Kolbe, Apostle of Our Difficult Age* (Boston: Daughters of St. Paul, 1982).

17. Nan C. Merrill, *Psalms For Praying: An Invitation to Wholeness* (New York: Continuum, 2000), Psalm 144, p. 299.

DAY SIX
Real Presence

With the gift of listening comes the gift of healing, because listening to your brothers or sisters until they have said the last words in their hearts is healing and consoling. Someone has said that it is possible "to listen a person's soul into existence."
—Catherine de Heuck Doherty[1]

Coming Together in the Spirit

In an age defining itself more and more in terms of efficiency, economy, speed and superiority, the human tends to get pushed aside. Even the message, "All of our representatives are currently busy...", is apparently considered to be too generous and is being replaced more and more by: "The information you are seeking can be obtained by visiting our web site...." The message behind these messages seems to be that humans get in the way and would better be replaced by machines talking to machines.

Those of us who grew up in awe and wonder at the marvel of being able to speak to someone miles away simply by talking into a telephone have adjusted somewhat to, "Please listen to the following menu," even to the point of being surprised if we should actually hear a human voice answer, "Hello, may I help you?"

Answering machines are here to stay, and they serve well as symbols of the time in which we live. In a world driven by a continually escalating economy, cost containment is certainly a goal worthy of pursuit and careful planning. Hand in hand with the increased importance of saving money is the necessity of saving time. Nouwen paints a vivid image of the extent to which our lives are dominated by the demands of time:

> In our contemporary society it often seems that not money but time enslaves us. We say, "I wish I could do all the things that I need to do, but I simply have no time. Just thinking about all the things I have to do today—writing five letters, visiting a friend, practicing my music, making a phone call, going to class, finishing a paper, doing my meditation—just thinking about these makes me tired." Indeed, it seems that many people feel they no longer have time, but that time has them. They experience themselves as victims of an ongoing pressure to meet deadlines, to be ready on time, or to make it on time. The most frequently heard excuse is, "I am sorry, but I have no time." The most common request nowadays is, "I know how busy you are, but do you have a minute?" And the most important decisions are often made over a quick lunch, or—to use an even more catching phrase—"while grabbing a bite." A strange sense of being hurried has entered into many people's lives. It seems as if the time in front of us gets filled up so quickly that we wonder, "Who or what is pushing me? It seems that I am so busy I have no time left to live." [2]

What is missing more and more from our lives is the life-giving gift of "Real Presence"—the gift that a human being gives in setting aside all other claims and urgencies in order to be fully present to another human being without measuring time. An inspiring example of this kind of presence can be found in the relationship that grew and matured over a number of years between Henri Nouwen and Adam Arnett. We will devote Day Six of our retreat to taking a closer look at this relationship and listening to what it might say to us about reclaiming our own humanity while giving due respect to another's.

Opening Prayer

> Come, Holy Spirit, ever one,
> With God the Father and the Son,
> It is the hour our souls possess
> With your full flood of holiness.
> Let flesh and heart and lips and mind
> Sound forth our witness to mankind
> And love light up our mortal frame
> Till others catch the living flame.[3]

RETREAT SESSION SIX

Henri Nouwen was not immune to the pressures of modern day living with its crowded schedules and busy signals. His secretaries reported he received an average of fifty requests a week for speaking engagements from continents all over the world. In *Wounded Prophet*, Michael Ford notes with a chuckle: "He would have agreed to everything were it not for friends who had his best interests at heart."[4]

As noted in our introduction, the story of how Nouwen came to find his final and true calling by serving as pastor to the L'Arche community of Daybreak is fully documented in his book, *The Road to Daybreak*. Here we will focus on the special relationship that developed between Nouwen and one of the most severely disabled persons he was assigned to care for at Daybreak: Adam.

Soon after his arrival at Daybreak Nouwen was given charge of Adam, who could not speak, feed or bathe himself. An epileptic from birth, he was subject to seizures which kept him continually in need of medication. At first Nouwen was anxious because waking Adam and walking him through his morning routine seemed to take so long. He confesses that he consistently tried to "hurry" Adam because he was preoccupied with getting back to his "important work"—his writing, his voluminous correspondence, phone calls to be made, lectures to be prepared, and personal projects to be pursued.

His coworkers challenged him: "Henri," they said to him, "We know you have important things to do, but nothing is more important than for you to slow down and take time to 'get to know Adam.'" Nouwen took the admonition to heart and began to take his relationship with Adam more seriously. So much so, that he came to look forward to being with Adam and began speaking gently and lovingly to him, even though Adam could not speak back to him. Over time, his hours with Adam became prayerful, reflective, and filled with a sense of being in the presence of the Holy. In turn, Henri became truly present to Adam.

In February of 1987, Nouwen was asked to give a lecture at Harvard, at St. Paul's Catholic Church, on the subject of peace. At first hesitant, Nouwen accepted the invitation and decided to build the entire talk around Adam. He began his talk by referring to Adam as "the silent spokesman of the peace that is not of this world." Without apology he described in detail the relationship that grew out of his caring for Adam and why he considered Adam a prophetic figure, a peacemaker in the truest sense of the word. What follows is an extended quote from the Harvard lecture. Readers will benefit by keeping in mind as they read, the theme guiding us in this retreat: "Reclaiming Our Humanity." Nouwen begins:

> After a month of working...with Adam, something started to happen to me that never had happened to me before. This deeply handicapped young man...started to become my dearest companion. As my fears gradually decreased, a love started to emerge in me so full of tenderness and affection that most of my other tasks seemed boring and superficial compared with the hours spent with Adam. Out of this broken body and broken mind emerged a most beautiful human being offering me a greater gift than I would ever be able to offer him. It is hard for me to find adequate words for this experience, but somehow Adam revealed to me who he was and who I was and how we can love each other. As I carried his naked body into the bathwater, made big waves to let the water run fast around his chest and neck, rubbed noses with him and told him all sorts of stories about him

and me, I knew that two friends were communicating far beyond the realm of thought or emotion. Deep speaks to deep, spirit speaks to spirit, heart speaks to heart. I started to realize that there was a mutuality of love not based on shared knowledge or shared feelings, but on shared humanity. The longer I stayed with Adam the more clearly I started to see him as my gentle teacher, teaching me what no book, school or professor could have ever taught me.

...Recently—during the writing of this story—Adam's parents came for a visit. I asked them: "Tell me, during all the years you had Adam in your home, what did he give you?" His father smiled and said without a moment of hesitation: "He brought us peace...he is our peacemaker...our son of peace."

Adam says to me, "Peace is first of all the art of being." I know he is right because after four months of being with Adam I am discovering in myself a beginning of an inner at-homeness that I didn't know before. I even feel the unusual desire to do a lot less and be a lot more, preferably with Adam.

Adam's peace is not only a peace rooted in being, but also a peace rooted in the heart. That true peace belongs to the heart is such a radical statement that only people as handicapped as Adam seem to be able to get it across! Somehow during the centuries we have come to believe that

what makes us human is our minds.
Many people who do not know any Latin
still seem to know the definition of a
human being as a reasoning animal:
rationale animal est homo (Seneca). But
Adam keeps telling me over and over
again that what makes us human is not
our minds but our hearts, not our ability
to think but our ability to love.

Let me say here that by heart I do not
mean the seat of human emotions in
contrast to the mind as the seat of human
thought. No, by heart I mean the center of
our being where God has hidden the
divine gifts of trust, hope, and love. The
mind tries to understand, grasp problems,
discern different aspects of reality, and
probe the mysteries of life. The heart
allows us to enter into relationships and
become sons and daughters of God and
brothers and sisters of each other. Long
before our mind is able to exercise its
power, our heart is already able to
develop a trusting human relationship. I
am convinced that this trusting human
relationship even precedes the moment of
our birth.

Here we are touching the origin of the
spiritual life. Often people think that the
spiritual life is the latest in coming and
follows the development of the biological,
emotional, and intellectual life. But living
with Adam and reflection on my
experience with him makes me realize
that God's loving spirit has touched us

long before we can walk, feel, or talk. The
spiritual life is given to us from the
moment of our conception. It is the divine
gift of love that makes the human person
able to reveal a presence much greater
than himself or herself.

The peace that flows from Adam's
broken heart is not of this world. It is not
the result of political analysis, round table
debates, discernment of the signs of the
times, or well-thought-out strategies. All
these activities of the mind have their role
to play in the complex process of
peacemaking. But they all will become
easily perverted to a new way of
warmaking if they are not put into the
service of the divine peace that flows from
the broken heart of those who are called
the poor in spirit.[5]

Adam Arnett died in February of 1996. Shortly after
Adam's death, Nouwen decided he would like to write a
book about Adam, patterning Adam's story on the life of
Jesus. He completed and sent a first draft to his publisher,
Robert Ellsberg of Orbis Books, with whom he
corresponded about revisions that would be necessary for
the book to be brought to publication. As it turned out,
Nouwen died suddenly on September 21, only months
after Adam's death, and the task of editing and completing
the book fell to Sue Mosteller, named literary executrix in
Nouwen's will. The book was published in 1997 under the
title *Adam, God's Beloved*. I think it appropriate that we sum
up these reflections on Real Presence with a quote from
this concluding passage in the book:

I have heard about and read about the life of Jesus, but I was never able to touch or see him. I was able to touch Adam. I saw him and I touched his life. I physically touched him when I gave him a bath, shaved him, and brushed his teeth. I touched him when I carefully dressed him, walked him to the breakfast table, and helped him to bring the spoon to his mouth. Others touched him when they gave him a massage, did exercises with him, and sat with him in the swimming pool and Jacuzzi. His parents touched him. Murray, Cathy, and Bruno touched him. That's what we did: touched Adam! And what is said of Jesus must be said of Adam: "Everyone who touched him was healed." (Mark 6:56)[6]

For Reflection

- *We have reviewed a portion of Nouwen's ministry under the heading of "Real Presence." Does this seem to diminish or expand in any way the manner in which you are accustomed to think of Real Presence? Is there some way you can think of bringing the concept of Real Presence to bear on your family life, on your relationship to others in the workplace, in the church or civic community to which you belong?*

- *In his book,* Adam, God's Beloved, *Nouwen casts Adam's life story within the framework of the story of Jesus, weaving it creatively to parallel Jesus' hidden life, his time of testing in the desert, his public life and ministry, his passion, death, resurrection, and finally the sending of his*

Spirit. Meditatively, review your own life story and, using your imagination, see what parallels might be found to link your story with the story of Jesus.

■ *Discuss with your friends or church community how the ideal of cultivating Real Presence can be maintained in a world preoccupied with the priorities of concern for security, economy, efficiency and technological advancement.*

Closing Prayer

Dear Lord...I think of the thousands of people suffering from lack of food and of the millions suffering from lack of love.... Isn't my faith in your presence in the breaking of the bread meant to reach out beyond the small circle of my brothers to the larger circle of humanity and to alleviate suffering as much as possible?

If I can recognize you in the Sacrament of the Eucharist, I must also be able to recognize you in the many hungry men, women, and children. If I cannot translate my faith in your presence under the appearance of bread and wine into action for the world, I am still an unbeliever.[7]

Notes

1. Catherine de Hueck Doherty, *Poustinia: Christian Spirituality of the East for Western Man* (Notre Dame, Ind.: Ave Maria Press, 1975).

2. *Clowning in Rome* (New York: Doubleday Image, 1979), pp. 94–95.

3. *Cistercian Hymnal.*

4. Michael Ford, *Wounded Prophet: A Portrait of Henri J. M. Nouwen* (New York: Doubleday, 1999), pp. 41–42.

5. The quotes from Nouwen's lecture at Harvard first appeared in *Weavings*, March–April, 1988, under the title: *The Peace That Is Not of This World*, and subsequently in my compilation, *Seeds of Hope: A Henri Nouwen Reader* (New York: Bantam Books, 1989), pp. 191–205, 256–261.

6. *Adam, God's Beloved* (Maryknoll, New York: Orbis Books, 1997), p. 127.

7. *A Cry For Mercy*, p. 72.

Day Seven
Reclaiming our Individuality

...[T]o this day in Italy children who received that caress on that night have felt entitled to pass on to their children, and they in turn to theirs, 'la carezza di Papa Giovanni.'
—Thomas Cahill[1]

In his biography of Pope John XXIII, Cahill tells the touching story of how the new pope, on the day after the opening of the Second Vatican Council appeared at his window at night to greet the fifty thousand people gathered singing in St. Peter's Square. Responding to the people's cheering enthusiasm, the pope told them to "go home, where they belonged, 'and give your children a caress. Tell them it is *la carezza del Papa*' (the caress of the Pope)." Many did just that, bringing the presence of Pope John to those who could not meet him personally.

Coming Together in the Spirit

As suggested in the introduction to our retreat, many would regard Nouwen's book, *The Return of the Prodigal Son*, as his most mature work. I have reserved comment on this book for the seventh and last day of the retreat because of the universal reach of the biblical story on which it is based and the ability of that story to shed light on the basic theme which has guided us in the preceding pages. As we conclude our reflections on that theme, Nouwen helps us to rediscover the meaning of our humanity in the light of one of the most moving stories in all classical and biblical literature.

Nouwen opens his book by placing before his readers the full text of the story as recorded in Luke's Gospel. He then proceeds to tell the reader how he came to his decision to write a book about it:

> A seemingly insignificant encounter with a poster presenting a detail of Rembrandt's *The Return of the Prodigal Son* set in motion a long spiritual adventure that brought me to a new understanding of my vocation and offered me new strength to live it. At the heart of this adventure is a seventeenth-century painting and its artist, a first-century parable and its author, and a twentieth-century person in search of life's meaning.[2]

That's what we are searching for in the pages of this retreat: a twentieth-century—actually now a twenty-first century—understanding of life's meaning in the light of the Gospel proclamation in the first century.

Opening Prayer

> *I kneel before you, God, my Father and my Mother. I put my ear against your chest and listen without interruption to your heartbeat. Then, and only then, can I say carefully and very gently what I hear. I know now that I have to speak from eternity into time, from the*

lasting joy into the passing realities of our
short existence in this world, from the house
of love into the houses of fear, from Your abode
into the dwellings of human beings. I am well
aware of the enormity of this vocation. Still,
I am confident that it is the only way for me:
looking at people and this world through
your eyes.[3]

RETREAT SESSION SEVEN

We concluded our survey of Nouwen's writings in the
opening pages of this retreat noting that Nouwen died of a
heart attack in Holland while en route to Russia. Dutch TV
had asked him to do a documentary on Rembrandt's
painting *The Return of the Prodigal Son,* which was housed
in the Hermitage in St. Petersburg.[4]

How Nouwen came to write the book is another story.
He first saw a copy of Rembrandt's painting when he
visited the L'Arche community in Trosly, France. He
relates in his introduction to the book how he discovered
it. He had gone to visit his friend, Simone, in her office. As
he approached, he noticed a large poster pinned on her
door. The image caught his eye immediately. Noticing
how moved he was by the painting, his friend remarked,
"Maybe you should have your own copy. You can buy it
in Paris."

It did not take Henri long to go shopping in Paris. So
taken was he by the depth and beauty of the painting in
the months following that he eventually flew to Russia
and arranged through a friend to have special access to
the original at the Hermitage. Permitted to sit before the
painting in the hall where it was on display, he spent two

days studying the figures in the portrait, taking note of the shifting play of the sunlight on its panoply of color, and pondering the meaning of it all. It was out of this total engagement with the painting that the book was born six years later.

While most of us who have read or heard the story tend to identify primarily, if not solely, with the younger son, Nouwen found himself identifying with all three of the major figures, and in the process, inviting his readers to expand their own understanding of the story.[5]

The Younger Son

The younger son's return takes place in the very moment that he reclaims his sonship, even though he has lost all the dignity that belongs to it. In fact, it was the loss of everything that brought him to the bottom line of his identity. He hit the bedrock of his sonship. In retrospect, it seems that the prodigal had to lose everything to come into touch with the ground of his being. When he found himself desiring to be treated as one of the pigs, he realized that he was not a pig but a human being, a son of his father. This realization became the basis for his choice to live instead of to die. Once he had come again in touch with the truth of his sonship, he could hear—although faintly—the voice calling him the Beloved and feel—although distantly—the touch of blessing. This awareness of and confidence in his father's love, misty as it may have been, gave him the strength to claim for himself his sonship, even though that claim could not be based on any merit.[6]

Often I have asked friends to give me their first impression of Rembrandt's *Prodigal Son*. Inevitably, they point to the wise old man who forgives his son: the benevolent patriarch.

The longer I looked at "the patriarch," the clearer it became to me that Rembrandt had done something quite different from letting God pose as the wise old head of a family. It all began with the hands. The two are quite different. The father's left hand touching the son's shoulder is strong and muscular. The fingers are spread out and cover a large part of the prodigal son's shoulder and back. I can see a certain pressure, especially in the thumb. That hand seems not only to touch, but, with its strength, also to hold. Even though there is a gentleness in the way the father's left hand touches his son, it is not without a firm grip.

How different is the father's right hand! This hand does not hold or grasp. It is refined, soft, and very tender. The fingers are close to each other and they have an elegant quality. It lies gently upon the son's shoulder. It wants to caress, to stroke, and to offer consolation and comfort. It is a mother's hand.

Some commentators have suggested that the masculine left hand is Rembrandt's own hand, while the feminine right hand is similar to the right hand of *The Jewish Bride* painted in the same period. I like to believe that this is true.

As soon as I recognized the difference between the two hands of the father, a new world of meaning opened up for me. The Father is not simply a great patriarch. He is mother as well as father. He touches the son with a masculine hand and a feminine hand. He holds, and she caresses. He confirms and she consoles. He is, indeed, God, in whom both manhood and womanhood, fatherhood and motherhood, are fully present. That gentle caressing right hand echoes for me the words of the prophet Isaiah: "Can a woman forget her baby at the breast, feel no pity for the child she has borne? Even if these were to forget, I shall not forget you. Look, I have engraved you on the palm of my hands."

...Is it too much to think that the one hand protects the vulnerable side of the son, while the other hand reinforces the son's strength and desire to get on with his life?[7]

[G]radually over the years I have come to know those hands. They have held me from the hour of my conception, they welcomed me at my birth, held me close to my mother's breast, fed me, and kept me warm. They have protected me in

> times of danger and consoled me in times
> of grief. They have waved me good-bye
> and always welcomed me back. Those
> hands are God's hands. They are also the
> hands of my parents, teachers, friends,
> healers, and all those whom God has
> given me to remind me how safely I
> am held.[8]

Contemplating the hands of the Father, Nouwen
recognizes that those hands are to become our own hands.
As children we are dependents and recipients. But
children must eventually grow up and become Father and
Mother:

> I could never have dreamt that becoming
> the repentant son was only a step on the
> way to becoming the welcoming father. I
> now see that the hands that forgive,
> console, heal, and offer a festive meal
> must become my own.[9]

> Indeed, as son and heir I am to become
> successor. I am destined to step into my
> Father's place and offer to others the same
> compassion that he has offered me. The
> return to the Father is ultimately the
> challenge to become the Father.[10]

We began this retreat with Henri Nouwen, a Roman
Catholic priest, with a quote from a self-styled secular Jew,
Jonathan Rosen. I can't think of a better way to bring the
retreat to a conclusion than by quoting again from Rosen's
book, *The Talmud and the Internet*. In Chapter Two of his
book, quoting another author, he describes the process of
how, in medieval Europe, a Jewish boy of five or six was
initiated into the study of the Torah:

"Early on the morning of the spring
festival of Shavuot (Pentacost [sic]),
someone wraps him in a coat or talit
(prayer shawl) and carries him from his
house to the teacher. The boy is seated on
the teacher's lap and the teacher shows
him a tablet on which the Hebrew alphabet
has been written. The teacher reads the
letters first forwards, then backwards, and
finally in symmetrically paired
combinations, and he encourages the boy
to repeat each sequence aloud. The
teacher smears honey over the letters on
the table and tells the child to lick it off."[11]

This is a beautiful image, a useful image. We should pour
honey on the Scripture texts Nouwen points out to us, as
well as those we have discovered on our own. We need to
"lick" them, savor them, ingest them, allow their
sweetness to penetrate our whole being until they become
a part of us. We too should inscribe the words on cakes
and eggs and teach our children to eat them, digest them,
until they become a part of their flesh and bone.

For Reflection

- *Reflecting on Rembrandt's painting, Nouwen notices
especially the hands of the Father. He notes: "Gradually
over the years I have come to know those hands." Have you
ever experienced the touch of hands such as these? Put
yourself in the place of the Younger Son. Kneel before the
Father and let those hands rest on your shoulders. Feel their
weight. The weight of forgiveness. The weight of total
acceptance, unconditional love. These hands welcome you
back into the family.*

■ *Look at your own hands. Is there someone in your life you find hard to forgive? Claim your power to forgive by mentally laying your hands on that person's shoulders, granting absolute, unconditional forgiveness. Forgive just as you have been forgiven.*

Closing Prayer

Prayer of Saint Francis

Lord, make me an instrument of your peace.
Where there is hatred, let me sow love.
Where there is injury, pardon;
Where there is doubt, faith;
Where there is despair, hope;
Where there is sadness, joy;
Where there is darkness, light.
O Divine Master, grant that I may not so much seek to be consoled, as to console;
Not so much to be understood, as to understand;
Not so much to be loved, as to love.
For it is in giving that we receive,
It is in pardoning that we are pardoned,
It is in dying that we are born again to eternal life.[12]

Notes

1. Thomas Cahill, *Pope John XXIII* (New York: Viking Penguin, 2002), p. 57.

2. Henri Nouwen, *The Return of the Prodigal Son* (New York: Doubleday, 1992), p. 3.

3. Adapted from *Prodigal Son*, p. 15.

4. Since I have already commented on the basic themes in Nouwen's book on the *Prodigal Son* in a previous volume, I refer my readers to that work and limit myself here to aspects of the story that tie in more directly with the theme we have been pursuing in this retreat: *Reclaiming Our Humanity*. See: *Henri Nouwen: In My Own Words*, Robert Durback, ed. (St. Louis: Liguori Publications, 2001).

5. *Prodigal Son*, p. 49.

6. *Prodigal Son*, p. 98–99.

7. *Prodigal Son*, p. 96.

8. *Prodigal Son*, p. 111.

9. *Prodigal Son*, p. 116.

10. *Prodigal Son*, p. 25.

11. Ivan Marcus, quoted by Jonathan Rosen, *The Talmud and the Internet* (New York: Farrar, Straus and Giroux, 2000), p. 25.

12. Prayer attributed to Saint Francis of Assisi.

Going Forth to Live the Theme

One of Nouwen's favorite images in his lectures and writing was the image of the clown. Invited in the late 1970s to spend a semester giving lectures to students at the North American College in Rome, he used the backdrop of the city of Rome, buzzing with tourists, pilgrims, artists, rich and poor, purse snatchers and church people of high rank and low, to build his lectures around the theme of circus, with clowns as the center of entertainment. He later published his reflections during this period in a book entitled *Clowning In Rome*.

He explains his choice of this image: "Clowns are not in the center of the events. They appear between the great acts, fumble and fall, and make us smile again after the tensions created by the heroes we came to admire. The clowns don't have it together, they do not succeed in what they try, they are awkward, out of balance, and left-handed, but...they are on our side.... The clowns remind us with a tear and a smile that we share the same human weaknesses."[1]

I think Henri Nouwen would applaud a contemporary clown who mirrors back to us the mixed blessings of technology and how we stumble and fall in our attempts to build a utopia of gadgets and conveniences, only to find ourselves facing monsters rising up in plumes of smoke out of the magic lanterns we have so cleverly crafted.

Points for Meditation in a Technological Age

We have taller buildings but shorter
tempers, wider freeways, but narrower
viewpoints.
We spend more, but have less. We buy
more, but have less.
We have bigger houses and smaller
families, more conveniences, but less time.
We have more degrees but less sense,
more knowledge, but less judgment,
More experts, yet more problems, more
medicine, but less wellness.
We drink too much, smoke too much,
spend too recklessly, laugh too little, drive
too fast, get too angry, stay up too late, get
up too tired, read too little, watch TV too
much, and pray too seldom.
We have multiplied our possessions, but
reduced our values.
We talk too much, love too seldom, and
hate too often.
We've learned how to make a living, but
not a life.
We've added years to life not life to years.
We've been all the way to the moon
and back
But have trouble crossing the street to
meet a new neighbor.
We conquered outer space but not
inner space.
We've done larger things, but not better
things.
We've cleaned up the air, but polluted
the soul.

We've conquered the atom, but not our
prejudice.
We write more, but learn less.
We plan more, but accomplish less.
We've learned to rush, but not to wait.
We build more computers to hold more
information, to produce more copies
than ever,
But we communicate less and less.
These are the times of fast foods and slow
digestion, big men and small character,
Steep profits and shallow relationships.
These are the days of two incomes but
more divorce, fancier houses, but
broken homes.
These are days of quick trips, disposable
diapers, throwaway morality, one night
stands,
Overweight bodies, and pills that do
everything from cheer, to quiet , to kill.
It is a time when there is much in the
showroom window and nothing in the
stockroom.[2]

We began our retreat by taking as our point of departure
the significant move of the editors of *Time* magazine in
bypassing the choice of "Man of the Year," to name the
winningest newsmaker of them all: The Machine of the
Year. We might wonder if there isn't a lurking danger that,
given our lifestyles today, anyone of us might find
ourselves eligible for being identified as a "machine of the
year." Throughout his writings Henri Nouwen teaches us
the disciplines we need to cultivate if we are to claim our
humanity and avoid becoming just one more cog in the
clutter of machines that now have such an impact on the
shaping of our lives.

The first discipline is to listen attentively to the voice that calls us "Beloved." By listening faithfully to this voice we discover not only our own truest identity, but how we are to relate to others around us who are also God's Beloved. In his book *Can You Drink The Cup?* Nouwen points out another discipline we need to cultivate if we are to grow to the fullest stature of our humanity: *looking critically at what we are living.*[3]

He tells the story of how at family festive gatherings before beginning the meal, his uncle presided over what became a formal ritual: standing at his place at the table, lifting his cup of wine and giving his personal appraisal of the quality of the vintage. With a touch of humor, Nouwen revisits the family scene:

> After the wine had been poured into the glasses, my uncle took his glass, put both of his hands around the cup, moved the glass gently while letting the aroma enter his nostrils, looked at all the people around the table, lifted it up, took a little sip, and said: "Very good...a very good wine...let me see the bottle...it must be a fiftier."

Nouwen continues: "This was my uncle Anton, my mother's oldest brother, priest, monsignor, authority in many things, good wines being one of them. Every time uncle Anton came to family dinners, he had a comment or two to make about the wine that was served. He would say, 'A full body,' or... 'Could be a little hardier,' or 'This is just good with roast,' or 'Well, for fish this is okay.'"

Nouwen concludes: "His criticisms were not always appreciated by my father, who provided the wine, but nobody dared to contradict him." Nouwen draws from this family cameo: "One thing I learned from it all:

drinking wine is more than just drinking. You have to know what you are drinking, and you have to be able to talk about it. Similarly, just living life is not enough. We must know what we are living. A life that isn't reflected upon isn't worth living. It belongs to the essence of being human that we contemplate our life, think about it, discuss it, evaluate it, and form opinions about it. Half of living is reflecting on what is being lived."

Holding the cup of life means looking critically at what we are living. This requires great courage, because when we start looking, we might be terrified by what we see. Questions may arise that we don't know how to answer. Doubts may come up about things we thought we were sure about. Fear may emerge from unexpected places. We are tempted to say: "Let's just live life. All this thinking about it only makes things harder." Still, we intuitively know that without looking at life critically we lose our vision and our direction. When we drink the cup without holding it first, we may simply get drunk and wander around aimlessly.

We often compare our lives with those of others, trying to decide whether we are better or worse off, but such comparisons do not help much. We have to live our life, not someone else's. We have to hold *our own* cup. We have to dare to say: "This is my life, the life that is given to me, and it is this life that I have to live, as well as I can. My life is unique. Nobody else will ever live it. I have my own history, my own family, my own body, my own character, my own friends, my own way of thinking, speaking, and acting—yes, I have my own life to live. No one else has the same challenge. I am alone, because I am unique. Many people can help me to live my life, but after all is said and done, I have to make my own choices about how to live."

It is hard to say this to ourselves, because doing so confronts us with our radical aloneness. But it is also a wonderful challenge, because it acknowledges our radical uniqueness.

I am reminded of Philip Sears's powerful sculpture of Pumunangwet, the Native American at the Fruitlands Museums in Harvard, Massachusetts. He stands with his beautifully stretched naked body, girded with a loincloth, reaching to the heavens with his bow high above him in his left hand while his right hand still holds the memory of the arrow that just left for the stars. He is totally self-possessed, solidly rooted on the earth, and totally free to aim far beyond himself. He knows who he is. He is proud to be a lonesome warrior called to fulfill a sacred task. He truly holds his own.

Like that warrior we must hold our cup and fully claim who we are and what we are called to live. Then we too can shoot for the stars![4]

The retreat ends here.
Go forth and…
Claim your humanity.
Your humanity.
Not someone else's.
You.
God's Beloved.

Notes

1. *Clowning in Rome* (New York: Doubleday, 1979), pp. 2–3.

2. This reflection by George Carlin, which I have renamed "Points For Meditation…" was taken from a printed flyer with the title, "A Wonderful Message." It is undated and no publisher is noted. I am indebted to my friend, Sr. Jeanne Koma, H.M., for calling it to my attention.

3. *Can You Drink The Cup?* (Notre Dame, Ind.: Ave Maria Press, 1996), pp. 25–26.

4. *Can You Drink The Cup?*, pp. 27–29.

Deepening Your Acquaintance

Internet

www.nouwen.net

Books by Henri Nouwen

Adam: God's Beloved. Maryknoll, N.Y.: Orbis Books, 1997.

Aging: The Fulfillment of Life. New York: Doubleday Image Books, 1974.

Behold the Beauty of the Lord: Praying with Icons. Notre Dame, Ind.: Ave Maria Press, 1987.

Beyond the Mirror: Reflections on Death and Life. New York: Crossroad, 1990.

Bread for the Journey: A Daybook of Wisdom and Faith. San Francisco: HarperSanFrancisco, 1997.

Can You Drink the Cup? Notre Dame, Ind.: Ave Maria Press, 1996.

— *Clowning in Rome: Reflections on Solitude, Celibacy, Prayer and Contemplation*. New Rev. Ed. New York: Doubleday, 2001.

Compassion: A Reflection on the Christian Life, coauthored with Don McNeill and Douglas Morrison. New York: Doubleday Image Books, 1982.

Creative Ministry. New York: Doubleday Image Books, 1971.

A Cry for Mercy: Prayers from the Genesee. Maryknoll, N.Y.: Orbis Books, 1981.

✓*Genesee Diary: Report from a Trappist Monastery.* New York: Doubleday, 1976.

Gracias! A Latin American Journal. San Francisco: HarperSanFrancisco 1983.

Heart Speaks to Heart. Notre Dame, Ind.: Ave Maria Press, 1989.

Here and Now: Living in the Spirit. New York: Crossroad, 1994.

In Memoriam. Notre Dame, Ind.: Ave Maria Press, 1980.

In the Name of Jesus: Reflections on Christian Leadership. New York: Crossroad, 1989.

The Inner Voice of Love: A Journey Through Anguish to Freedom. New York: Doubleday, 1996.

Intimacy: Essays in Pastoral Psychology. San Francisco: HarperSanFrancisco, 1969.

Jesus and Mary: Finding Our Sacred Center. Cincinnati: St. Anthony Messenger Press, 1993.

A Letter of Consolation. San Francisco: HarperSanFrancisco, 1982.

Letters to Marc About Jesus. San Francisco: HarperSanFrancisco, 1988.

Life of the Beloved: Spiritual Living in a Secular World. New York, Crossroad, 1992.

Lifesigns: Intimacy, Fecundity and Ecstasy in Christian Perspective. New York: Doubleday Image Books, 1986.

The Living Reminder: Service and Prayer in Memory of Jesus Christ. 1971. New Revised Edition. San Francisco: HarperSanFrancisco, 1981.

Love in a Fearful Land: A Guatemalan Story. Notre Dame, Ind.: Ave Maria Press, 1985.

Making All Things New: An Invitation to the Spiritual Life. San Francisco: HarperSanFrancisco, 1981.

✓ *Our Greatest Gift: A Meditation on Dying and Caring.* San Francisco: HarperSanFrancisco, 1994.

✓ *Out of Solitude: Three Meditations on the Christian Life.* Notre Dame, Ind.: Ave Maria Press, 1974.

Path Series: The Path of Waiting/The Path of Freedom/The Path of Power/The Path of Peace. New York: Crossroad, 1995.

✓ *Reaching Out: The Three Movements of the Spiritual Life.* New York: Doubleday, 1975.

✓ *The Return of the Prodigal Son: A Story of Homecoming.* New York: Doubleday, 1992.

The Road to Daybreak: A Spiritual Journey. New York: Doubleday, 1988.

Sabbatical Journey: The Final Year. New York: Crossroad, 1997.

Thomas Merton, Contemplative Critic. 2nd ed.: Liguori, Mo.: Triumph Books, 1981.

Walk With Jesus: Stations of the Cross. Maryknoll, N.Y.: Orbis Books, 1990.

The Way of the Heart: Desert Spirituality and Contemporary Ministry. New York: Ballantine Books, 1981.

With Burning Hearts: A Meditation on the Eucharistic Life. Maryknoll, N.Y.: Orbis Books, 1994.

With Open Hands. 2nd ed. Notre Dame, Ind.: Ave Maria Press, 1972, *Revised Edition,* 1995.

The Wounded Healer: Ministry in Contemporary Society. New York: Doubleday Image Books, 1972.

Collections (Readers)

Bence, Evelyn, ed. *Mornings With Henri J. M. Nouwen.* Ann Arbor, Mich.: Servant Publications, 1997.

Dear, John, ed. *The Road to Peace: Writings on Peace and Justice.* Maryknoll, N.Y.: Orbis Books, 1998.

Durback, Robert, ed. *Seeds of Hope: A Henri Nouwen Reader.* 2nd ed. New York: Doubleday, 1997.

Garvey, John, ed. *Henri Nouwen, The Modern Spirituality Series.* Springfield, Ill.: Templegate Publishers, 1988.

Greer, Wendy Wilson, ed. *The Only Necessary Thing: Living a Prayerful Life*. New York: Crossroad, 1999.

Johna, Franz, ed. *Show Me the Way: Readings for Each Day of Lent*. New York: Crossroad, 1992.

Jonas, Robert A., ed. *Henri Nouwen: Writings*. Maryknoll, N.Y.: Orbis Books, 1998.

Jones, Timothy, ed. *Turn My Mourning Into Dancing*. Nashville: W Publishing Group, 2001.

Laird, Rebecca and Michael J. Christensen, eds., *The Heart of Henri Nouwen: His Words of Blessing*. New York: Crossroad, 2003.

O'Laughlin, Michael, ed. *Jesus: A Gospel*. Maryknoll, N.Y.: Orbis Books, 2001.

Books About Henri Nouwen

Beumer, Jurjen. *Henri Nouwen: A Restless Seeking for God*. New York: Crossroad, 1997.

Ford, Michael. *Wounded Prophet: A Portrait of Henri J. M. Nouwen*. New York: Doubleday, 1999.

LaNoue, Deirdre. *The Spiritual Legacy of Henri Nouwen*. New York: Continuum, 2000.

Porter, Beth with Susan M. S. Brown & Philip Coulter. *Befriending Life: Encounters With Henri Nouwen*. New York: Doubleday, 2001.

Bread for the Hungry   GIA
(Most Requested - Music For The Spirit)

Audio

Desert Spirituality & Contemporary Ministry – 2 cassettes

The Lonely Search For God – 2 cassettes

The Return of the Prodigal Son – 3 cassettes

A Spirituality of Waiting – 2 cassettes

Audiobooks

Nouwen books read by Murray Bodo, O.F.M. Available from St. Anthony Messenger Press, 1-800-488-0488.

Video

The following videos are available from Daybreak Publications, 1-800-853-1412, www.nouwen.net:

Straight to the Heart: The Life of Henri Nouwen (60 minutes)

Angels Over The Net (30 minutes)

With Burning Hearts (25 minutes)

A Tribute to Henri Nouwen: Cross Currents Interview
(56 minutes)